NEW
HOLLAND

First published in 2004 by New Holland Publishers
London • Cape Town • Sydney • Auckland
www.newhollandpublishers.com

86 Edgware Road
London W2 2EA
United Kingdom

80 McKenzie Street
Cape Town 8001
South Africa

14 Aquatic Drive
Frenchs Forest
NSW 2086, Australia

218 Lake Road
Northcote, Auckland
New Zealand

ISBN 1 84330 597 6

Publishing managers: Claudia dos Santos, Simon Pooley
Commissioning editor: Simon Pooley
Publisher: Mariëlle Renssen
Designer: Trinity Loubser-Fry
Editor: Claudia dos Santos
Cartographers: Genené Hart, Nicole Engeler
Illustrator: Adam Carnegie
Picture Research: Karla Kik
Production: Myrna Collins
Proofreader: Alfred LeMaitre

Reproduction by Hirt & Carter (Cape) Pty Ltd
Printed and bound in Singapore by
Tien Wah Press (Pte) Ltd

2 4 6 8 10 9 7 5 3 1

ENDPAPERS *Passengers on the Bolan Mail.*
HALF TITLE *The Desert Express in the Namib.*
TITLE PAGE *The Bernina Railway near Ospizio.*
OPPOSITE *The Union Limited at Groot Brakrivier.*
FOLLOWING PAGES *QJ class 2-10-2 Nos. 6996 and
7143 on the Si Ming Yi horseshoe viaduct, Jitong Line.*

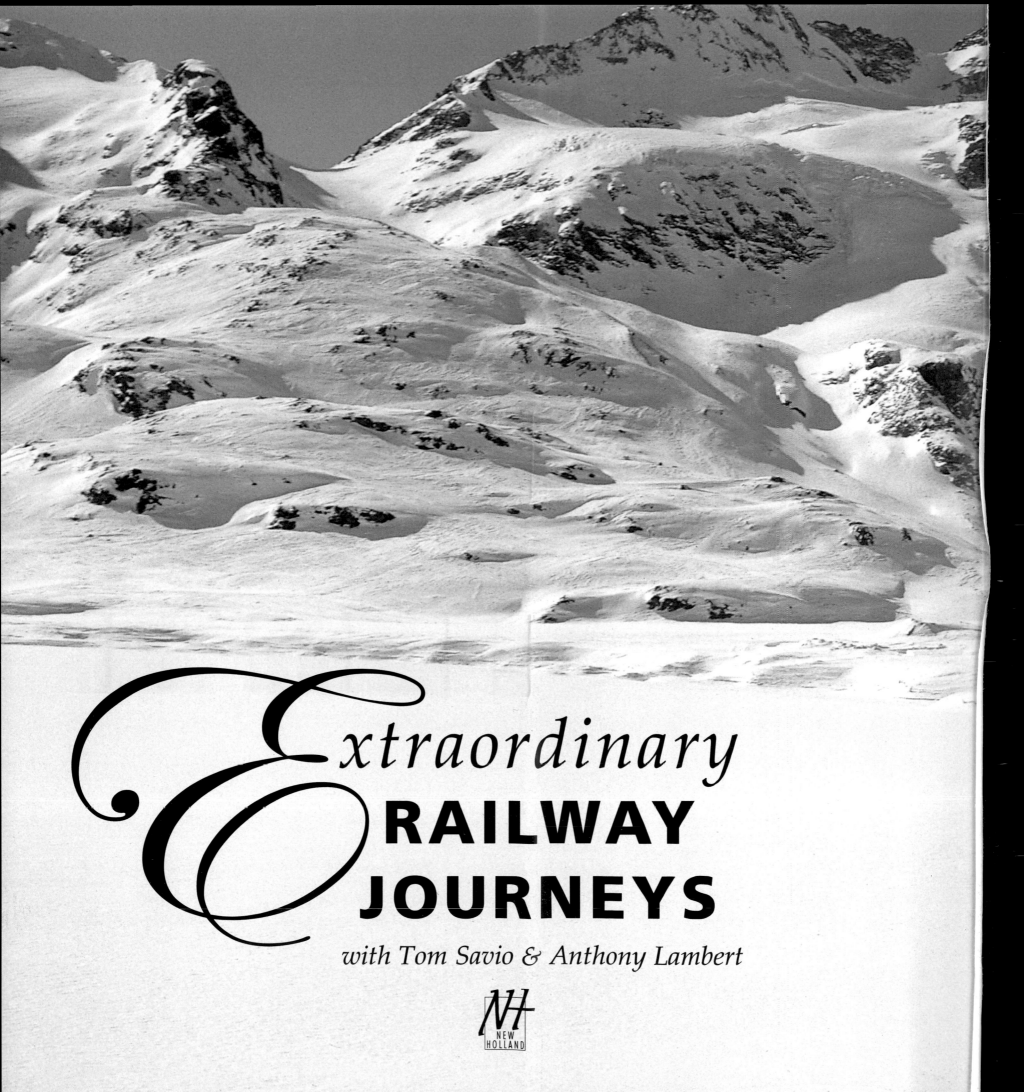

Extraordinary RAILWAY JOURNEYS

with Tom Savio & Anthony Lambert

NH
NEW
HOLLAND

Extraordinary
RAILWAY
JOURNEYS

CONTENTS

INTRODUCTION

Extraordinary Railway Journeys

My extraordinary railway journey began at the age of four, when a bravely borne trip to the hospital to mend my broken arm was rewarded with a toy train. That harrowing, but, in hindsight, fortuitous event was followed by outings with Dad chasing after the last steam engines, then careers as stationmaster, railway museum curator and rail travel writer, my 'coronation' as The Railway Baron during a memorable evening in a Kamloops, British Columbia bar, and ultimately the immortalization of my Rail Baron persona as 'public art' in the forecourt of my town's new tramway station.

In terms of world history, railways are nearly immortal themselves. They first appeared in ancient times as rutted guideways for carts and chariots. By the Middle Ages, miners were pushing mineral-laden wagons along crudely hewn wooden rails. But it wasn't until the Industrial Revolution that railways made their appearance as a system of public transport for passengers and goods, and the world has never been the same since.

If a single person can be credited with sparking the Industrial Revolution that engendered the railways, it would be Abraham Darby of Coalbrookdale, England. In 1709, he perfected the smelting of unlimited quantities of iron using coke – made

RIGHT *Paddington Station in the mid-1950s, showing the ornately decorated clock and the first-floor offices from which the stationmaster enjoyed a superb view over the concourse.*

8

from plentiful coal – instead of charcoal, which was solely dependent on Britain's dwindling forests, and consequently in short supply. Suddenly, there was a plenitude of strong, durable iron (and later its derivative, steel), for a wide variety of new industrial, agricultural and household applications, as well as steam locomotives and the rails on which to run them.

On a recent train trip to London's Euston Station, I noted the name of one locomotive, *Abraham Darby*. When the engine driver joined me on the platform, I asked him if he knew who Darby was. He thought for a moment and said, 'I think he plays for Manchester United'. When I told him that Darby was, in large part, responsible for the railways we had just travelled he said, 'But sir, every schoolboy knows George Stephenson was the father of railways'.

Indeed, when George Stephenson opened the Stockton & Darlington on 27 September 1825 in the North of England, it was the first public railway to use the newly perfected steam locomotive to speedily haul (at 13 kph; 8 mph!) goods and passengers over rails made of iron. Trains ventured beyond the gates of industrial estates and became public conveyances in their own right, transporting raw materials, manufactured goods, agricultural products, mail, parcels, newspapers and the working class cheaply and predictably over a mushrooming network of all-weather railways. Long-distance commerce was stimulated; knowledge, culture and the gene pool were disseminated. Even high-speed communications became commonplace, utilizing the telegraph wires that were strung along the railways to safely dispatch trains. The railways were the greatest invention of the Industrial Revolution, and they propelled it ever faster and farther.

Soon a multitude of lines competed fiercely in Britain for the meagre commerce of even the smallest village. Scotland was the last frontier for Britain's railway builders. By the late 19th century tracks were driven across the magnificent moors and mountains of the Highlands, employing the latest technology, including the pioneering concrete viaducts of Sir Robert 'Concrete Bob' McAlpine, sire of the most scenic railway in Britain – the West Highland Line.

ABOVE *This 1889 poster advertises the splendid journey of the Orient Express from Paris to Constantinople (now Istanbul).*

Although Stephenson netted the garland for the first steam railway, his star was nearly eclipsed by a little man with a great big cigar and a splendid name: Isambard Kingdom Brunel, builder of the grandest railway of all – the Great Western – that ultimately linked London with the Cornish Riviera resorts. The GWR (or God's Wonderful Railway to its acolytes), being nearly innocent of curves and grades on its main stem, became the high priest of the pre-eminent deity of the Industrial Revolution – Speed. The fastest train on the railway synonymous with speed was the record-setting Cornish Riviera Express, a holiday institution that still departs from Brunel's magnificent Paddington Station in spite of the circumstances Britain's railways find themselves in today.

As in the infamous tulip speculation of 17th-century Holland, reality inevitably caught up with Britain's bloated railway network. Rail barons were ruined and lines abandoned, absorbed, amalgamated, grouped, nationalized and then inexplicably re-privatized. But the railways' darkest hour struck in 1963 at the hands of the relentless Dr. Beeching, the late Chairman of British Rail. In an ill-conceived scheme to make the railways serve profit instead of public, Beeching arbitrarily amputated the branch lines that generated traffic for the system as a whole. Today, as many of Britain's railways lie in utter disarray, Dr. Beeching endures as the 'Moriarty of railways'.

Fortunately, Britain exported the Industrial Revolution and the railways that drove it. Consequently, there are extraordinary and successful railways to ride around the globe. At the top of Europe, in Norway, the railway's metallic tentacles wind their way across the Arctic Circle in the eerie light of the midnight sun on the Oslo–Bodø Line. Across the Irish Sea, between Dublin and Tralee, Ireland's simple but hospitable trains roll through gently green landscape beneath Waterford-crystalline skies. Although railways were originally the servants of industry, the Swiss perfected them as alpine touring trains. On the serpentine Gotthard Pass Route, between Zurich and Milan, trains trace a path among the glaciated pinnacles that once knew Hannibal's elephants. Serving the heart of Switzerland, the Zurich–Montreux Golden Pass Route uses a variety of connecting modes to showcase its exquisite mountains, lakes and villages, culminating with an awesome descent to the shores of Lake Geneva – enjoyed by tourists from the glazed nosecone of the train. However, the stupendous Bernina Railway surpasses all other rail treks in Heidi-land. From the ski slopes of St Moritz to the palm trees of Tirano, Italy, the Bernina combines the best of the fabled Glacier Express route with its own gravity-defying engineering – including a unique sculpture-studded spiral viaduct – on the climb to the perpetual snows at the crest of the Continent.

Not all extraordinary train trips are travel epics however; there are many great little railway journeys. Le Petit Train Jaune, the 'Canary', runs through the sunny valleys of the Pyrenees, dubbed 'the centre of the world' by Salvador Dali. The island of Sardinia hosts a bouquet of quaint railways in the care of snorting 'puffing billys' that pull their trains across carpets of springtime flowers and around the cliffs above the Mediterranean Sea. Another network of diminutive steam trains chuffs in the Harz Mountains of Germany. On its climb to the summit, the Brocken Railway treads through the dark green forests that recall German mythology and Romanticism, home to witches, warlocks and Goethe's Faust. However, its chunky tank engines are relatively modern contraptions built in an East German engine shop with a decidedly unromantic, proletarian name – the Karl Marx Locomotive Works.

At the dawn of the railway age, Britain and Europe were already urbanized and had efficient, though slow, canal systems to serve industry and commerce. It was the undeveloped continents of Africa, Asia, Australia and the Americas that benefited most from railways. This new transportation infrastructure allowed the easy exploitation of natural resources, promoted agriculture, encouraged tourism and established towns and cities. America's transcontinental railroad, traversed by the California Zephyr, was the physical manifestation of westward migration and arguably the single most important business enterprise in US history. The majestic Alaska Railroad, route of the Denali Star, and the historic White Pass & Yukon Route were pioneer railways, the one to foster settlement in 'Seward's Icebox', and the other to transport 'stampeders' to the last great Golconda – the Klondike Gold Rush. The railway to sublime Machu Picchu was built to tap Peru's agricultural riches, but thrives today on tourist traffic not even dreamed of before Hiram Bingham 'rediscovered' the cloud city of the Incas.

The surviving steam railways in the Ukraine's historic Crimea, like those of the other former Soviet republics, are among the most heavily trafficked in the world, and strategically vital to the vast landmass that is still without a paved highway extending all the way between the Baltic and Bering seas.

Along with the English language and Common Law, one of the greatest 'civilizing' instruments of the British Empire was the construction of efficient, punctual and tidy railways. India was the jewel in the Imperial Crown, and its railways were doted upon by the British like no others in the Empire. There are few traditions more redolent of the gilded Raj than the seasonal railway migrations from India's steaming, polluted cities to the cool, serene hill stations. Steam trains transported the elite and their retinues to the healthful climes of Coimbatore in the Blue Hills, and the line to storied Simla at the threshold of the mighty Himalayas. However, some of today's most evocatively named trains, like the Bolan Mail and the Sind Express, are associated with the military railways built from broiling Karachi, in today's Pakistan, to the rugged snowy heights along the restless Afghan frontier.

An ocean and a continent away, in Australia's tropical Deep North, the intrepid British surveyed a railway through the malarial cane fields of Cairns, spiralling upwards over waterfalls to Kuranda's rainforests and across the balmy Tablelands for the gold mines of Mt. Surprise and beyond. This is the route of the silvery Savannahlander, a self-propelled Art Deco motor-car train from which the kaleidoscopic views can be enjoyed, in typically informal Aussie style, up front with the driver.

LEFT *A level (grade) crossing sign in Peru.*

THE AMERICAS

USA AND CANADA

The Royal Canadian Pacific
The White Pass & Yukon Route
The Denali Star
The California Zephyr

PERU

The Machu Picchu Vistadome

LEFT *The California Zephyr near Burns, Colorado.*

The Royal Canadian Pacific

THE GOLDEN CROWSNEST PASS EXCURSION (CANADIAN ROCKIES CIRCUIT)

BY TOM SAVIO

ROUTE *Calgary–Banff–Lethbridge–Head-Smashed-In Buffalo Jump–Crowsnest Pass–Cranbrook–Fort Steele–Banff–Calgary (Alberta and British Columbia, Canada).*
DISTANCE *1035km (643 miles).* **DURATION** *The Golden Crowsnest Excursion includes an evening reception and two nights at the historic (former Canadian Pacific) Fairmont Palliser Hotel in Calgary: the tour is 5 nights, 6 days (return); the train trip alone is 3 nights and 3½ days.* **GAUGE** *1435mm (4ft 8½in).*

As we perused the railway exhibits in the Canadian Museum of Civilization in Gatineau, Quebec, my companion wanted to know why I was so fascinated by the Canadian Pacific Railway (CPR). Standing by an exhibit of model railway carriages, I compared the dour, dark green cars of Canadian National Railways to the deep, rich Tuscan red coaches favoured by its arch rival, Canadian Pacific. The CPR was an imperial institution that literally built Canada – its transcontinental line was stipulated in the treaty that welcomed British Columbia (BC) into Confederation. CPR's celebrated family of posh trains, *White Empress* ocean liners and château-style hotels comprised part of the 'All-Red Route', the English-speaking travel network named for the red tint that once delineated the British Empire on world maps.

By the end of the 20th century, the CPR was hauling only freight, its passenger trains had been absorbed by VIA Rail Canada, and it had amicably divorced itself from its ship and hotel subsidiaries. All that remained of the once-magnificent fleet of Tuscan carriages was a handful of vintage 'business cars' (directors' saloons) for its officers.

In the 1990s, a controversial economic theory swept the industrialized world: each segment of a business was expected to pay for itself as though it were completely independent from the resources of the mother company. Consequently, such cherished conveniences as railway business cars (that were still used for inspections, and as venues for fêting commodity chieftains and chiefs of state) were expected to bear the full cost of their operation.

The Canadian Pacific business-car fleet was no exception. However, they were the wards of an exceptional railwayman, R.J. 'Rob' Ritchie, the President and Chief Executive Officer. Mr Ritchie, a visionary railway marketer and unabashed rail romantic, managed to save the magnificent land yachts and contribute to the railway's bottom

LEFT *Mount Stephen, named for the first president of the Canadian Pacific Railway, rises above the Royal Canadian Pacific and the town of Field, BC, at the base of the Big Hill – Kicking Horse Pass.*

line by chartering them for a limited number of public excursions over what the CPR hailed, in the 19th century, as 'the most picturesque route in the world'.

For the first time, the splendid mahogany-and-walnut carriages that hosted the world's glitterati for over 80 years, including generations of the Royal Family and the John Kennedys, were now available to discerning travellers and aspiring railway barons. The cars were painstakingly restored in the CPR shops, their brass platform railings were burnished, the nickel and art-glass fixtures polished, and their pantries stocked with crested bone china and the monogrammed silverware from the vaults that had once supplied the railway's deluxe trains, hotels and ocean liners. Mr Ritchie placed the carriages in the charge of his personal business-car staff and Managing Director, David Walker, his grain marketing guru and the genial host of innumerable business car soirées. The train was christened the Royal Canadian Pacific, but is affectionately called 'Mr Ritchie's Train' on the CPR. What had previously been one of the most exclusive trains in the world made its public début in June 2000.

The Royal Canadian Pacific rolled out from the Canadian Pacific Pavilion, its new gilded-age-style train shed adjoining the Fairmont Palliser Hotel, the former Canadian Pacific property in Calgary, Alberta. Upfront rumbled a brace of restored Art Deco diesel locomotives, dressed in the original Tuscan red livery that once pulled The Canadian, CPR's premier streamliner.

The itinerary, dubbed the Golden Crowsnest Pass Excursion, featured a 1035km (643-mile), four-day, three-night circuit of the Rocky Mountains. It followed CPR's transcontinental mainline over Kicking Horse Pass, then returned via rugged Crowsnest Pass on a line that had not seen a passenger train since 1964.

The train consisted of the carriages: *Assiniboine*, Mr Ritchie's personal car built in 1929; *Killarney*, used on the Prince of Wales' Royal Train of 1919; *Van Horne*, named for Sir William C. van Horne, KCMG, the expatriate American who sired the CPR empire; *Royal Wentworth*, which conveyed King George VI and Queen Elizabeth on the Royal Train of 1939, and the present Queen Elizabeth and Prince Philip; and *Mount Stephen*, favoured by Sir Winston Churchill, for whom a cosy smoking room was installed – the 'Churchill Cubby'.

I have been a guest on board the Royal Canadian Pacific on several occasions, following different itineraries since the train can be chartered over the entire CPR system from New York and Montreal to Vancouver, BC. During my Golden Crowsnest Excursion we headed west from Calgary, Alberta, which is the CPR's headquarters and the energy and ranching centre of Canada. We crossed the wide prairies and followed the Bow River into Banff National Park, climbing a thousand feet as we cruised past the resort town of Banff nestled in the Rocky Mountain peaks, and home to the celebrated Banff Springs Hotel.

When Van Horne pushed the CPR across the Rockies, he soon realized that the route linking Montreal with Vancouver across a wild and unsettled continent lacked sufficient passenger and freight traffic to make it a going concern. Consequently, he began to sell homesteads to eastern Canadians and European immigrants and established a chain of grand resort hotels, beginning with the Banff Springs, to lure tourists to the 'Canadian Pacific Rockies'. My CPR *Annotated Time Table* for the 1911 season assured prospective patrons that the Banff Springs was '...the most beautifully situated and luxuriously comfortable mountain hotel in the world'.

The Canadian Rockies are somewhat lower than their American counterparts, but their jagged and glaciated peaks appear taller because they soar a mile straight up from the railway. When I was stationmaster in a small university town in California, a graduating senior from Austria wanted to buy a ticket to Colorado to see 'the legendary Rockies' before she returned to her homeland. I told her that the legendary Rockies were in Canada, not Colorado, and sold her a ticket to Banff.

We followed the broad arcs of the Bow River through the mountain-ringed meadows and around Morant's Curve. For over 40 years, Nicholas Morant, OC, was the CPR's Special Photographer. His photos, including some from this location, were reproduced on Canadian

coins, banknotes, postage stamps, posters, menus, travel brochures and in countless magazines, etching an indelible image of Canada's outstanding natural beauty on the world's psyche. In addition to its deluxe resorts, the Canadian Pacific Railway built a network of beautiful small lodges and bungalow camps in scenic and remote locations such as Emerald Lake. The RCP's passengers joined Château Lake Louise naturalist Bruce Bembridge on a casual forest trek along the lake. Afterwards, when we returned to the train, we were greeted with tangy Caesars, a delicious and uniquely Canadian restorative.

CAESAR À LA CANADIAN PACIFIC

Rub glass rim with lime and dip in celery salt to form a salted rim.

Over ice cubes, add one dash of Tabasco pepper sauce, two dashes of Worcestershire Sauce, and salt and pepper to taste.

Add 227ml (8fl oz) Clamato juice and 28ml (1fl oz) Grey Goose Vodka.

Garnish with celery stalk and a slice of lime.

(For the equally delicious *Caesar à la Railway Baron* substitute Vodka with Cuervo Gold Tequila.)

The Château Lake Louise is one of my favourite hotels, not only for its magnificent view of a glaciated cirque reflected in the lake, but also for its sheer isolation. The great white castle looks as if one of the CPR's fabled White Empress liners had docked along the shore. An interesting nature hike around the shores of Lake Louise is planned for future excursions in lieu of the Emerald Lake stop. The CPR wrote of the lake, in its 1911 timetable '...bear[ing] the liquid music, the soft colour notes of its name into the realm of the visible'.

ABOVE *The RCP crosses the High Level Bridge at Lethbridge, one of the longest and highest trestle structures in the world.*
OPPOSITE *This image shows the train on Morant's Curve, west of Banff, which is named in honour of Nicholas Morant OC, the official photographer of the Canadian Pacific Railway for over 40 years.*

The Holy of Holies of the Canadian Pacific Railway is the Big Hill. Between the Great Divide and Field, BC, the railway descends nearly 305m (1000ft) down Kicking Horse Pass to the base of Mount Stephen. The dramatic view of the glaciered peaks above the train to the left, and the deep, narrowing valley of the Kicking Horse River below the roadbed to the right, is one of the finest in the entire railway world.

The first rail line through Kicking Horse Pass had an unwieldy 4.5% (1 in 22) grade, four steam locomotives were necessary to lift passenger trains up the Big Hill, and even then they were on the verge of slipping their driving wheels. The line was improved in 1909, when the unique Spiral Tunnels opened. By using a maze of looping tracks and corkscrew tunnels beneath Cathedral Mountain and Mount Ogden the grade was reduced to a manageable 2.2% (1 in 45).

At Golden, BC, the train trundled south onto the gentler tracks of the Windermere Subdivision, which haven't seen a passenger train since 1961 when old Mixed Train No. 806 plied its rails with freight, parcels and the occasional passenger. We ran through the peaceful, gentle valley of the headwaters of the Columbia River, protected by the peaks of the Selkirk and Purcell ranges. I spent the rest of the day sitting on the rear platform watching the bald eagles soar above us, and moose, beaver and salmon splash in the river. Whenever I put my field glasses down, I found that my Caesar had been refreshed – like a fine home, beverages come gratis on Mr Ritchie's Train.

Dinner on the RCP is unlike any I have had in a normal dining car. Business cars are configured differently than conventional passenger cars, and they are individual self-contained trains in their own right.

A train travelling downhill faces a unique challenge in stopping, as depicted in many silent-screen one-reelers. The RCP's vintage 'heavyweight' carriages weigh in at 100 tons each, so their brakes, while more than ample to retard the train's downward momentum, gave off such a haze of foul brake-shoe smoke that it sent those on the open platform scurrying into the air-conditioned comfort of the *Mount Stephen*. It occurred to me that the only problem with our otherwise perfect passage was that we were going in the wrong direction! If the itinerary were in a clockwise direction, our stalwart engines would have less of a challenge going up the Big Hill, and Banff, Canada's Vail, would be the ideal punctuation to end the trip. The view ascending the Big Hill would build to a natural climax, and the brake-smoke nuisance would vaporize. Later that afternoon, David Walker and I discussed the concept in the Churchill Cubby over a couple of Mr Ritchie's Montecristo Habanas. Ultimately, a clockwise itinerary was adopted for future Golden Crowsnest excursions.

Generally, each 24m (80ft) car has a galley, pantry, bunks for the staff, spacious cabins with en-suite showers and facilities for guests, a dining room with a large wooden table for meals and business meetings, and a lounge that faces an open platform used for track inspection, or – on the RCP – for viewing the scenery. Meals are served with all guests seated around one table. When the RCP is booked to its capacity of 32, two adjoining cars are set.

In the business car tradition, meals on the RCP are personalized to the desires of the clientele. Upon booking, passengers' preferences are solicited. Within practicality, these guide the menus created by Swiss-born Maitre d'train Morgan Burgess, and Chefs de cuisine Pierre Meloche, Denis Sirois and the brothers Alain and Eric Maheux. I requested trifle, a dessert practically unknown in California, but still a traditional treat in English-speaking Canada; it was the best I ever had. Dinners begin with cocktails at 7pm and usually end at midnight. Everyone is dressed to the nines and dines on CPR specialities like herb-crusted lobster tails, cashew-crusted tiger prawns, Australian rack of lamb. Everything is prepared from scratch in the *Mount Stephen*'s diminutive galley as the train is rolling. Meals become house parties with all the guests swapping tales, and gregarious David Walker, master of ceremonies, leading party games over dessert and aperitifs. The train is parked each evening to accommodate those guests who, unlike railway barons, do not sleep well on moving trains. Our first night was on a siding in the village of Invermere, BC, near spring-fed Lake Windermere, the source of the Columbia River.

The next morning, we motored to Fort Steele Heritage Town, a late 19th-century frontier historic site. The prospect of becoming a railway centre led to the development of Fort Steele in 1897, but when the CPR ultimately chose Cranbrook as its regional headquarters, Fort Steele's fortunes dimmed. Like a latter-day Brigadoon, the town went slowly to sleep, to be awakened 60 years later as a provincial park, with many of its original buildings intact and featuring a museum railway. Life sounded idyllic in the valley of the Columbia 100 years ago, until our guide recounted the rustic side of dentistry that relied, at times, on the curative properties of a carpenter's hammer and nails. After a frontier lunch in Mrs. Pou's old boarding house we made for the comparative metropolis of Cranbrook to visit the Canadian Museum of Rail Travel. Under restoration was a full complement of carriages from the CPR's premier Trans-Canada Limited of the early 20th century. Car interiors were so ornate they resembled the lobbies of movie palaces. By comparison, the RCP's business cars, from roughly the same era, were markedly restrained.

A notable exhibit was the original *Strathcona*, a rare, all-bedroom executive night car, and the former running mate of RCP's *Mount Stephen*, an executive day car without cabins. *Strathcona* was donated to the museum by the Conklin & Garrett Circus, who acquired it years before from the CPR. To take its place and provide additional cabins for heavily booked trains, RCP reconfigured a lowly rules instruction car into a posh all-bedroom sleeper. It was named, appropriately, after N.R. Crump, who, in his 52-year career, rose through the ranks from the humblest of railway crafts – engine-wiper – to president of the CPR.

We returned to the RCP at a remote siding and then played hopscotch with a procession of loaded and empty coal trains through the

twists and turns of fabled Crowsnest Pass. Crowsnest coal and prairie grain are the principal commodities on the CPR. At the summit, with an elevation of 1344m (4410ft), we settled in for the night. Dinner was followed by a live classical guitar and violin recital.

The following morning we rolled down from the Rockies to the high prairie and boarded a motor coach bound for Head-Smashed-In Buffalo Jump, a UNESCO World Heritage Site. Some 5500 years ago, the Blackfoot First Nations used this funnel-shaped terrain to stampede buffalo (bison) over the cliff. Carcasses were processed into food, clothing and shelter by the hunting camp below the precipice. It was a very carefully choreographed harvest, using the natural holding pens to limit the kills to just the number needed at the time. Another nearby landmark, this time from the Railway Age, is CPR's High Level Bridge

at Lethbridge, the longest and highest railway trestle of its type in the world. Hidden by the rolling prairie until you are practically on it, the mile-long span drapes between the bluffs, 96m (315ft) above the Oldman River, like a gigantic spider web. We sailed across it en route to our last night's stop in the small agricultural town of Okotoks. Next morning we would end our journey in Calgary.

As our final dinner wound down, I looked at the last drops of wine in my glass and saw the same deep, rich tone used on our Tuscan red carriages. No expense had been spared in building the original CPR coaches. They were crafted entirely of teak and then varnished, not painted. Over time, the varnish had mellowed to a rich dark red, coining the railway term 'varnish' for the finest passenger trains. In the early 20th century, when the railway introduced steel passenger cars, they were painted CPR's own shade of Tuscan red to blend seamlessly with the accompanying teak carriages, a tradition that continues with the Royal Canadian Pacific today.

FAR LEFT *A portrait of the crew on a RCP 'Rare Mileage' special charter.*
LEFT *A sleeping car cabin of the newly commissioned N.R. Crump mirrors the elegance of the RCP's historic business cars.*
ABOVE *Dressed in historic garb, naturalist Bruce Bembridge and a fellow passenger plot the RCP's course beneath Alberta's Selkirk Range.*

The White Pass & Yukon Route

SKAGWAY (ALASKA) TO CARCROSS (CANADA)

BY TOM SAVIO

ROUTE *From Skagway to either White Pass Summit (Alaska), or Lake Bennett (British Columbia, Canada), and return. One-way ticket available for trekkers or bus connectors to Whitehorse, Yukon Territory. Occasionally to Carcross and return.* **DISTANCE** *The original railway was 177km (110 miles), but the tracks now in service are only between Skagway and Carcross (108km; 67 miles).* **DURATION** *(approximately) Skagway–Summit: 1³/₄ hours one way; 4 hours return. Skagway–Lake Bennett: 3 hours one way; 8 hours return, including 2-hour layover for guided tour. Skagway–Carcross: 5–6 hours one way; 10–12 hours return.* **GAUGE** *914mm (3ft).*

In its heyday, the White Pass & Yukon Route (WP&YR) linked Skagway in Alaska with Whitehorse in the Yukon Territory (YT), Canada, by 177km (110 miles) of rails just 914mm (3ft) wide. Its extraordinary legend and magnificent scenery, however, overshadowed its modest proportions by far. It was a railway born of hard drink, hard times and dreams of gold.

On 14 July 1897, the SS *Excelsior* steamed into San Francisco harbour carrying half a million dollars' worth of gold from the Klondike diggings in Canada's Yukon. Two days later, the steamer *Portland* docked in Seattle laden with gold worth over a million dollars. Seattle newspapers ran large banner headlines proclaiming **GOLD! GOLD! GOLD!** A special supplement was printed about the new eldorado and, in an unprecedented act of civic boosterism, mailed to every post office and library in the country. The last great gold rush of the North American frontier had begun.

There were only three practical routes to the Klondike from Seattle, the closest port. The easiest, longest and most expensive was entirely by ship, halfway around Alaska and up the Yukon River to its confluence with the Klondike. The other routes included a steamer trip through the protected waters of the 'Inside Passage' to Skagway or Dyea, Alaska, followed by overland treks over Chilkoot Pass or White Pass to Lake Bennett, from where stampeders floated down the Yukon to the Klondike. Most chose the latter options – travelling the overland routes – because they were cheaper and faster.

Against this frenzied background, prospectors considered several alternatives. Cableways were tried, but they had limited capacity. Toll roads were unsuccessful, because they could not obtain franchises from the disinterested government thousands of miles away in

LEFT *On its way to Lake Bennett, a WP&YR train heads north after leaving Fraser, BC. With the rugged White Pass behind it, the train will follow the valleys for the remainder of its run.*

Washington, DC. And a railway up the sheer rockface of the Coast Range, 38km (24 miles) to the 896m (2940ft) summit, seemed utterly impossible.

Long before the gold rush, Captain 'Billy' Moore had dreamed of a railway over White Pass, 183m (600ft) lower than the more treacherous Chilkoot Pass. In 1887, Moore and a Tagish aboriginal, Skookum Jim, one of the original discovers of the Klondike gold fields, blazed a trail up White Pass that appeared suitable for a railway. At the base of the trail, on the Lynn Canal, Moore pitched a tent and staked a claim on what would someday become Skagway (Tagish for Windy Place). At first Moore had little success enlisting investors in his railway scheme, but 10 years later the gold rush was on. Skagway had become a city of 15,000 stampeders who demanded a railway.

Construction lagged until the Close Brothers contracting firm in Great Britain commissioned a feasibility study from Sir Thomas Tancrede. After hiking the rugged route he rejected the railway outright, but a chance meeting in a Skagway bar changed his mind. In a long night of persuasion, celebrated Canadian railway contractor Michael J. Heney sold Tancrede on the idea, and by morning they were toasting the new endeavour. Eventually, three 'paper railways' were formed: the Pacific & Arctic Railway & Navigation Co. in Alaska, the British Yukon Railway Co. in British Columbia, and the British Columbia Yukon Railway Co. in the Yukon Territory. Together they formed the White Pass & Yukon Route ('Wait Patiently & You'll Ride' to veteran sourdoughs).

From the beginning, 914mm (3ft) narrow gauge track was chosen over the world standard of 1435mm (4ft 8½in), because it required only a 3m (10ft) right of way, instead of the usual 4.5m (15ft), allowing for cheaper and faster construction. This was especially true for a route that had to be carved out of solid granite.

Construction commenced on 28 May 1898, and at its height employed a workforce of over 30,000 labourers. Prone to striking and not immune to gold fever, they often vanished with the railway's tools to mine likely prospects. The original route staked by Captain Moore

N

CARCROSS

Lake Bennett

CANADA

0   20 km

10 miles

Bennett

C

Fraser

White Pass Summit

Glacier

SKAGWAY   Clifton
Denver

Taku Glacier

USA

ABOVE *The glaciered peaks of the Sawtooth Mountains rise above the diminutive narrow gauge right-of-way that was blasted into the granite by fearless trackmen dangling from ropes, on the White Pass & Yukon Route – Scenic Railway of the World.*

and Skookum Jim was followed. However, unlike most railways, there was no open land leading to the mountains, where the tracks could climb gently up by looping around. Consequently, the railway began its climb in Skagway and didn't stop until the summit, using a very steep 3.9% (1 in 26) maximum grade. The vertical sheer drop was so severe that much of the right-of-way and the face of the tunnel were cleared with dynamite charges set by workers suspended on ropes from above. Haste was imperative, and work continued all winter in temperatures as low as -34°C (-30°F). The most significant structure on the line was the Dead Horse Gulch cantilever bridge. Built in 1899, the 65.5m-high (215ft) structure was a world record for its type at the time.

By the time completion of the railway was celebrated on 29 July 1900, the gold rush was over. Fickle stampeders were sailing down the Yukon to Nome, Alaska, where gold nuggets were literally strewn on the beach. The WP&YR turned its attention to transporting less exotic minerals, including zinc, lead and asbestos, and generally developing the Yukon interior, amassing an armada of river steamers

and, later, road and air services. In World War II it prospered as the railhead for the Alaska Highway – originally a military road spurred by the Japanese invasion of Alaska's Aleutian islands. After the war, heavy mineral traffic compelled the rebuilding of the WP&YR to contemporary railway standards and bypassing Dead Horse Gulch Bridge with a second tunnel. In 1982, when mineral prices dropped precipitously and the parallel all-weather Klondike Highway opened, all railroad services were abandoned. The spectacular WP&YR could have been torn up had it not been for a seemingly unrelated event half a world away.

In October 1985, after Palestinian operatives hijacked the Mediterranean liner *Achille Lauro*, the cruise ship industry searched for calmer waters. They began cruising the Inside Passage to Alaska and calling at historic Skagway. Fortunately, the charming 19th-century wooden passenger coaches and quaint steam and diesel locomotives had only been dozing in the railway yards, and the magnificent scenery had stayed the same. The WP&YR was reopened (ultimately to Carcross, formerly known as Caribou Crossing), and became the cruise lines' most popular shore excursion.

It was a cool summer's day when I boarded the WP&YR parlour car *Lake Bennett*, a 120-year-old veteran from the Arizona & New Mexico Railway, at the Skagway depot. Steam locomotive No. 73, built in 1947 by Philadelphia's Baldwin Locomotive Works, sighed impatiently, waiting for another run up White Pass. Typically, trains run as far as Summit or Lake Bennett. The railway has several itineraries designed to dovetail with the schedules of the cruise ships moored in Skagway harbour, but occasionally it hosts charter trains and self-propelled railbus excursions. Mine was a special run 40km (25 miles) further along the scenic shore of the lake to the current end-of-steel at Carcross.

The longest straight track on the WP&YR is the 1.6km (1-mile) segment between Mileposts 3 and 4. From there it follows a succession of cliff-hanging curves to the summit. Some 3km (2 miles) further upline is the Denver flagstop, where the train will stop for trekkers visiting the Denver Glacier, or for campers who have reserved an overnight stay in a former WP&YR caboose maintained by the US Forest Service. At Clifton we passed beneath an immense overhang. Across the gorge by the Klondike Highway, a gigantic sign proclaimed 'On to Alaska with Buchanan'. George Buchanan was an American coal merchant who operated a programme for disadvantaged boys in the 1920s and '30s, leading them on summer excursions into the Alaskan wilderness. The sign, repainted by generations of graduates, is now maintained by the community.

Soon we bridged the 549m (1800ft) Pitchfork Falls and slowly passed Black Cross Rock. Remarkably, only 35 workers were killed during the two-year race to dynamite the railway out of solid granite, without toeholds and while working in winter. Black Cross Rock is a memorial to the fallen, including the two still buried beneath the boulder that was blasted loose from the cliff above. At Glacier, Milepost 14, we stopped to allow No. 73 to replenish its tender with

a drink of pure glacial water from Laughton Creek. Next we crawled along a narrow shelf with a sheer 153m (500ft) drop, and a spindly wooden trestle that plunged into a tunnel – not the kind of train trip where people talk to each other. All eyes were on the scenery.

The granite peaks on White Pass have been likened to the buttresses of a gigantic cathedral with the train snaking around and through them, giving rise to the White Pass' motto: 'Scenic Railway of the World'. Beyond the tunnel is Inspiration Point with its panorama of the jagged Sawtooth Mountains and the Lynn Canal in the distance. Here is another memorial, this time to the 3000 pack animals that were crushed by their burdens, or flogged to death by crazed stampeders. Bones still litter the floor of Dead Horse Gulch below the landmark cantilever bridge.

The summit of White Pass at 879m (2885ft) marks the United States–Canada boundary and the Arctic–Pacific watershed. Nearby Summit Lake is the headwaters of the Yukon, where cruise ship trains turn back for an easy daytrip from Skagway, but 6.5km (4 miles) further upline is the actual railway summit of 896m (2940ft). At Fraser, BC, we stopped by the original hundred-year-old, all-in-one water tank, railway station and section (maintenance) house, while Canadian Customs inspected the train before it whistled off for Lake Bennett. In its boom as winter camp during the gold rush, Lake Bennett housed 7,000 impatient stampeders who stripped the forests of timber to build their river craft while waiting for the spring ice break-up. The WP&YR has a combination station and eating-house here that once served hearty meals to track workers, train crew and passengers. Today, boxed lunches are served.

The last 40km (25 miles) to Carcross follows Lake Bennett, a great inland sea replete with white caps. Our train rounded a final bend and crossed over the railway's original 1901 swing bridge, a timber tour-de-force. Carcross, with a year-round population of 400, lies at the southern tip of the Yukon in a valley of exquisite beauty, framed by

ABOVE *The WP&YR clings to its track, cut from solid rock in 1900, and crosses the Pitchfork Falls as it climbs to the summit at White Pass. This is the most spectacular part of the route.*

pale lavender mountains and bordered by clusters of fuchsia fire-weed. The hamlet treasures its 1909 two-storey railway station that serves today as visitors' centre and museum for tourists off the Klondike Highway and the occasional train.

It is ironic that this magnificently wild land, once so feverishly mined for its subterranean riches, and then heroically conquered by White Pass & Yukon Route, was the real treasure all along.

ABOVE *During the centennial celebration in Carcross (July 2000), WP&YR tour guide Brendan Heney, great-nephew of the railway's builder Michael J. Heney, re-enacted the driving of the golden spike that completed the line.*

RIGHT *A WP&YR train exits Tunnel 1 and immediately crosses a wooden trestle on the return trip to Skagway, Alaska.*

BELOW *Former WP&YR caboose No. 905 now serves as a cabin for trekkers and is maintained by the US Forest Service at the Denver flagstop, Alaska.*

The Denali Star

FAIRBANKS TO ANCHORAGE, ALASKA

BY STEVE BARRY

ROUTE *Fairbanks–Denali National Park–Anchorage, Alaska.* **DISTANCE** *573km (356 miles).*
DURATION *12 hours (one way). Overnight stops at Denali National Park and Talkeetna are optional for the*
Alaska Railroad portion of the train, but included if riding with the cruise lines. **GAUGE** *1435mm (4ft 8½in).*

Among all the US states, Alaska stands out as the last frontier. Separated from the 'Lower 48' by Canada, this wilderness remains wild with abundant resources. But a ribbon of steel leaves Alaska's largest city and winds northward for over 573km (356 miles) through some of the most spectacular scenery and wildlife-filled forests. This is the Alaska Railroad, home to the Denali Star.

Alaska has become a favourite destination for cruise ships – which parade past the glaciers and visit the small coastal towns – but much of its beauty is far away from the water in the interior. To bring visitors to this part of the state, three cruise companies have purchased their own private passenger cars that ride behind the Alaska Railroad's own cars on the Denali Star, thus creating four self-contained trains that move along the railroad as one unit, powered by a single set of locomotives.

Sorting out the train from front to rear, you start out with a set of the Alaska Railroad's attractive yellow-and-blue diesel locomotives. Behind these you have the Denali Star, made up of the Alaska Railroad's own passenger cars, dome cars and dining cars. (Since the Denali Star makes its run entirely during the day, there are no sleeping cars on the train. Cruise lines offering multi-day packages stay in five-star hotels along the way.) Coupled

LEFT *The Denali Star makes its first stop since leaving Fairbanks, arriving at the Denali National Park. From here, passengers can take wildlife tours into the park's interior.*

behind the Alaska coaches are two double-decked dome cars – known as Wilderness Express and owned by Royal Celebrity, a company jointly owned by cruise ship operators Royal Caribbean and Celebrity. Next on the train are cars owned by the Holland America Line and operated as the McKinley Explorer. At the very rear of the train are cars owned by Princess and known as the Midnight Sun Express. Like the Wilderness Express cars, those of the McKinley Explorer and Midnight Sun Express are double-decked with a large viewing area on the top level and a dining room on the lower level. The top observation level features glass that curves to the middle of the ceiling, allowing for easy viewing of even the highest mountains.

While the Denali Star itself (the Alaska Railroad portion of the train) provides for an outstanding travel experience, the trip is made extraordinary if you ride with one of the cruise lines. The advantages of riding with Royal Celebrity, Holland America or Princess are numerous. Their railcars are more luxurious and their dome windows are kept clean. The food service in these cars rivals the quality of meals you'd expect from their ocean-going counterparts. The cruise lines provide seamless integration of the train ride and any off-train activities, should you decide to ride the Alaska Railroad in segments. And each provides an onboard host who will stay with your tour group for the entire trip, giving you a friendly face to go to in the event of any problems. Additionally, the hosts are well versed in Alaska lore and sightseeing, and are skilled at spotting wildlife from the train.

There is nothing wrong with riding the Alaska Railroad portion of the train, however. The coaches are clean, though far less luxurious than the cruise cars, and decent meal service is provided. If you want to ride the train's entire run from Fairbanks to Anchorage in one day, then you have to ride in the Alaska Railroad part of the train, as the cruise tours all feature stopovers at Denali National Park or Talkeetna (usually both). If you want the flexibility of determining your own itinerary, then the Alaska Railroad provides the easiest scheduling as well as the best value for money.

Now that I have presented all the options available for riding on the Alaska Railroad, it's time for the journey. The scenery gets better as you go from north to south, so it is recommended that you start your trip at Fairbanks. For those doing Alaska as a combination rail/water package, starting at Fairbanks allows for getting the more strenuous parts of the trip over first (the long flight from anywhere to Fairbanks, plus staying in different hotels each night while you are on the railroad portion of the trip) – once you reach the south end of the line and your cruise ship, you are ready to sleep in the same room for several nights.

Fairbanks is the northern end of the Alaska Railroad main line (and indeed the northernmost main line terminus in North America). The downtown has a 1950s look about it; most modern amenities are located outside this area. The station was adequate for the Denali Star before tourism discovered Alaska, but now cruise ship cars occupy the short platform in front of the building while the railroad's own cars are loaded from along the street one block away. A new station is planned, however. Fairbanks has the widest temperature range of any major US city, with summertime temperatures hitting 32°C (90°F) and sinking below -40° in winter.

Just after 8am the train is away from the Fairbanks station, heading south. After passing through the rail yards, the scenery opens up into grassy fields along the grounds of the University of Alaska. But civilization is soon left behind as the train heads into the scrubby spruce and aspen woods of central Alaska, where the vegetation is sparse due to permafrost. Riding in the cruise cars, an extravagant breakfast is served in the lower level of each dome car as the train heads south. After breakfast you may want to ride on the open observation platform, or just settle back into your dome seat. This part of Alaska is 'The Land of the Midnight Sun' where sunset in the long days of summer occurs around midnight. In fact, for over two months of the year it never gets dark as the sun never sets far below the horizon. Sunrise before 3am can be a bit unnerving for some – your watch indicates that it is bedtime, but your brain tells you it can't be, because the sun is still high in the sky. Nonetheless, the bountiful light allows for seeing

ABOVE *Fairbanks is the northernmost point on any North American main line. From here the Denali Star begins its southward journey.*
OPPOSITE *The Denali Star crosses the Tenana River on the Mears Memorial Bridge on its southbound run from Fairbanks.*

Alaska's wonders with extensive tours after dinner, if one desires.

Continuing south, the forest is interspersed with marshlands. The only signs of civilization are occasional hunting villages scattered along the railroad and a crossing of the Parks Highway. The Parks Highway is the main (well, only) auto and truck route to Fairbanks from the south. Roughly parallel to the Alaska Railroad all the way from Anchorage, it is usually several miles away and out of sight.

The first major town encountered by the southbound train is Nenana, and it's a good idea to begin making your way to the observation platform as the Denali Star approaches it. The train will turn east to follow the north bank of the Tanana River before heading south to cross the waterway on the Mears Memorial Bridge, a through-truss structure, and at 213m (700ft) the longest span in Alaska. At the north end of the bridge is the spot where US President Warren G. Harding drove in the golden spike that marked the completion of the Alaska Railroad on 15 July 1923. Look out the right side of the train and you'll see the town of Nenana down below; a sharp observer will pick out the railroad station along the banks of the Tanana River. One might wonder why the station is located so far from the main line. The answer is, it isn't. After crossing the Mears Bridge the railroad makes a 180-degree horseshoe to the right while descending a 1% (1 in 100) grade. At the end of the horseshoe, the train turns 90 degrees to the left (now heading west) and is running at river level along the banks of the Tanana and past the railroad station! The station now houses a little railroad museum, and the Denali Star no longer stops here.

Nenana marks the confluence of the Tanana and Nenana rivers and is home to an unusual competition each year. Contestants guess the exact day, hour, minute and second when the ice floes on the Nenana will break apart each spring, with the winner collecting a healthy cash prize. Sophisticated monitoring equipment is located here, and the headquarters of the competition can be seen from the train between the tracks and the Tanana River. After leaving town, the Denali Star continues south by following the course of the Nenana.

The next point of civilization is at Clear Site, home of a US Air Force base, where passengers may get their first glimpse of North America's highest mountain, rising 6194m (20,320ft). Known by most as Mount McKinley, Alaskans refer to it by its aboriginal name: Denali (The Great One). The mountain is the centrepiece of Denali National Park, which encompasses an area roughly a third of the size of Switzerland.

Now it's just before lunch, and the passengers in the domes are treated to one of the little-known wonders of Alaska, the Nenana River Canyon. Accessible only by rail, the canyon is an unstable geological area where earthquakes (albeit mostly minor tremors that go unnoticed by the general public) are a daily occurrence. Two short tunnels are traversed at Garner and Moody before the tracks pass under the Parks Highway and begin a climb into Denali National Park. At noon the train comes to a stop at the station located within the park, and most cruise passengers disembark for wildlife tours. The train trip resumes the next day at noon when the next southbound Denali Star passes through.

Immediately after leaving the Denali Park station the train swings across Riley Creek Trestle, second highest on the railroad. En route through the park it is not uncommon to see moose, bear, elk, Dall sheep and other wildlife. This is the Yanert Valley. The three mountains sticking up from the floor are known as the Pyramids, reminiscent of their Egyptian counterparts. From here to Talkeetna is the scenic heart of the railroad, with glacier-capped mountains and lake vistas at every turn. It's back to the open observation deck again when the train crosses Hurricane Gulch bridge, the highest on the line at 90m (296ft) above the river. The Talkeetna Mountains dominate most views from the train, with Denali – clearly the largest – standing off by itself.

Anchorage are finally reached. Unlike the 1950s look of Fairbanks, downtown Anchorage is modern, mostly due to the levelling of the entire city by a massive earthquake in 1964.

Twelve hours after leaving Fairbanks, the Denali Star stops at Anchorage station. The Alaska Railroad continues another 183km (114 miles) to Seward, port-of-call for cruise ships. The Denali Star doesn't cover this scenic line, but there is a connecting rail passenger service.

Alaska, the 49th state admitted into the United States of America, is truly the nation's last frontier. It is a state that should be 'experienced' rather than just visited, and the Denali Star provides the best opportunity to do just that. Board the train and take in the scenic splendour, but take the time to get off at Denali National Park and Talkeetna to visit the people and see what makes Alaska so special.

ABOVE *Moody Tunnel marks the southern end of the Nenana River Canyon. Passengers have spent the last two hours enjoying scenery that can only be seen from the train.*
LEFT *Minutes south of the Denali Park station, the Denali Star crosses the 174m (570ft) Riley Creek Trestle.*
BELOW *The long, combined passenger train steadily climbs the hills on its approach to the Denali National Park station. The Denali Star's yellow-and-blue cars are located behind the Alaska Railroad locomotives, with the double-deck cruise line cars at the rear.*

The next stop along the route is Talkeetna, a small town that has tried to retain its charm despite the incursion of the tourist industry. Talkeetna is the base for climbers heading for Denali, and has an air service to fly climbers and tourists onto the mountain. But Talkeetna's greatest claim to fame is that it was the model for the town of Cicely, Alaska, which featured in the US television show *Northern Exposure*. The modern five-star hotels that cater to cruise patrons were all built outside of town, and shuttle buses from the hotel only go to the town line, so all tourists have to explore the town on foot, keeping auto and bus traffic off Talkeetna's streets. Southbound out of Talkeetna, it isn't long before the suburbs of

The California Zephyr

CHICAGO TO SAN FRANCISCO BAY AREA, USA

BY TOM SAVIO

ROUTE *Chicago (Illinois) to Emeryville, San Francisco Bay Area (California).* **DISTANCE** *3923km (2438 miles).*
DURATION *3 days, 2 nights (eastbound or westbound).* **GAUGE** *1435mm (4ft 8½in).*

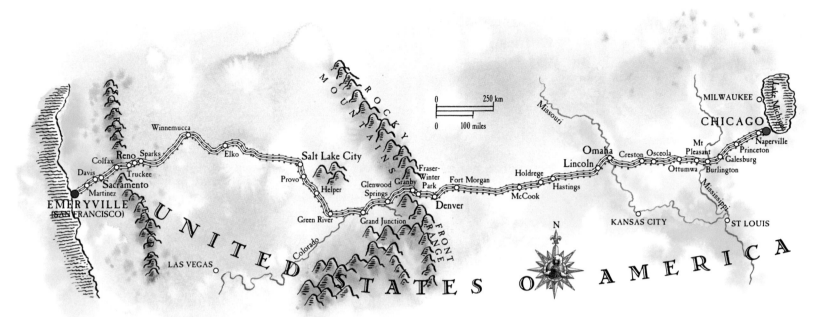

The California Zephyr, named for the mythological god of the west wind, is an American classic. There is no better way to experience the country's triumphs, many scenic treasures, its hubris and tragedies than from the panoramic windows of this train as it rolls across the heartland from Chicago to California.

The original California Zephyr, or CZ, had its debut in 1949 during the optimistic years following World War II – a time of small-town America – before television, Interstate highways and jet travel homogenized the country. Three connecting railroads, the Burlington, Rio Grande and Western Pacific, inaugurated a new streamlined passenger train linking the country's commercial capital, Chicago, Illinois, with San Francisco and the beguiling California lifestyle some 3923km (2438 miles) to the west. It competed successfully with faster trains on busier routes, because the scenery on the CZ's meandering line through the Rocky Mountains, the Sierra Nevada and the canyons of Colorado and Utah was the best.

Without any hope of luring time-sensitive business travellers who provided most passenger train revenue in the days before routine air travel, CZ's management, in a stroke of genius, promoted the train as a family holiday 'land cruise', thus pioneering the cruise-train concept that has since been adopted by the Venice Simplon-Orient-Express and other modern deluxe trains. A fleet of glass-domed cars, or Vista Domes, was commissioned from the trendsetting Budd Company. The cars, with evocative names like *Silver Banquet*, *Silver Sky*, and *Silver Planet*, were clad in polished stainless steel, and had

LEFT *The California Zephyr glides out of Chicago, leaving behind the canyons created by modern skyscrapers, and heads for scenic splendours of a different kind in the natural canyons carved by the Colorado River.*

elevated seating so passengers could enjoy the view from the domes. The California Zephyr's ad men went full-steam (or diesel in this case), and the public's imagination ran wild – it became what the dean of railroad PR men, Arthur Lloyd, was fond of calling 'America's most talked about train'.

Then in the latter 1950s, the villains who stood to profit by robbing the public of civilized travel – the petroleum, trucking, construction and auto industries – persuaded the federal government to build the Interstate Highway System. The handwriting was on the station wall, and one by one the streamliners yielded to the automobile. The death knell was the whoosh of a Boeing 707. The CZ fared better, but the financially weak Western Pacific opted out in 1970. The Burlington and Rio Grande continued a through service over the Southern Pacific Railroad's Donner Pass route.

In 1971, those who hadn't been swayed by the 'Autopia' flim-flam – rail passengers, environmentalists, train buffs, towns bypassed by the Interstate highways, rail unions, and African-American railroaders (passenger trains were the largest employers of Blacks) – persuaded the federal government to create Amtrak (from 'American' and 'track'). Eventually, all the railroads relinquished their money-losing passenger trains to the 'government entity', and a new *Amtrak California Zephyr* was born in 1985, using modern Superliner double-deck cars, including a stunning wall-to-ceiling glass-sided Sightseer Lounge. This was the train I boarded in Chicago Union Station on a glorious autumn afternoon.

Chicago traces its history to 1673, when the French explorers Marquette and Joliet located a portage on the Des Plaines River, where the Great Lakes, the Great Plains and the Mississippi River Valley converge. The city emerged as America's trading and transportation centre: beef, pork and grain from the heartland moved east, while settlers, farm implements and manufactured goods moved west. Chicago became the greatest railroad hub in the world, and today, it's Amtrak's hub as well.

Leaving Chicago Union Station, the city quickly receded behind the CZ's red marker lights, its trademark skyscrapers looking square-shouldered and triumphant. Highballing down the centre of the former Burlington (now Burlington Northern Santa Fe) triple-track, we roared past commuter trains on one track, and double-stack container trains on the other. Over these same tracks in 1934, the Burlington's first *Zephyr* broke the world record on a 1610km (1000-mile) non-stop, dawn-to-dusk dash from Denver to the Century of Progress International Exposition in Chicago. Radio stations transmitted live mile-by-mile broadcasts from the observation car, and newsreel aeroplanes kept pace overhead. Today, *Little Zip*, as she was nicknamed, ironically sits on a plinth in the automobile parking garage of the Chicago Museum of Science and Industry.

We quickly traded Chicago's smart suburbs for the golden wheat fields, red barns and silos of the Great Plains. This immense grassy habitat, rich with wild flowers, is the world's breadbasket, because its relatively temperate climate assures reliable harvests year after year. Chicago architect Frank Lloyd Wright celebrated this unassuming landscape with the spare horizontal lines of his prized Prairie-style homes.

At sunset we crossed the Mississippi River at Burlington, Iowa, from whence the railroad acquired its name. Back in the 19th century, nothing fired the imagination of youngsters along the Mississippi more than the big white stern-wheelers that resembled wedding cakes floating on the river – until the railroads asserted their legal rights to bridge the Mississippi, and the heyday of the riverboats finally gave way to the Railway Age.

A young woman boarded at Burlington and sat opposite me in the dining car. She was travelling to a new job in Denver and took the train instead of an aeroplane because, as she put it, 'Burlington is a long way to the nearest airport. Then it's a puddle-jumper east to Chicago, followed by a flight west to Denver, ending with a long taxi ride to downtown Denver, all at exorbitant cost. So, I hopped onboard Amtrak at the depot and will be in downtown Denver tomorrow morning, saving a lot of money and eating a lot better than on the plane.' Of course, dining onboard Amtrak's California Zephyr is not like it was in the original *Silver Banquet* dining car. Then, the tables were set with silver, fine china and fresh carnations, exuberant waiters

ABOVE *The California Zephyr on its climb towards Moffat Tunnel at Crescent, Colorado.*
OPPOSITE *The Front Range of the Rockies bursts into colour each autumn as the aspens glow gold. The westbound Zephyr twists and turns on its climb to the Continental Divide.*

were at your service and the menu boasted 'Mountain Trout served everyday in the dining car'. Amtrak's menu was less appealing than that of a chain restaurant and the waiters were aloof, but the steak was good, and fresh carnations still graced the tables.

After dinner, I retired to my sleeping car cabin. The sleeping car is a truly unique travel experience – miniature rooms with hideaway beds and storage nooks, with the world flying by their picture windows. Although long-distance train trips were common by the mid-19th century, nighttime travel was uncomfortable, unsanitary and anything but private until George Mortimer Pullman leased his luxurious *Palace Cars* to the railroads. Civilized drawing rooms by day, they became posh hotels at night thanks to heavy curtains and convertible beds. In the 1920s, 100,000 passengers slept on board Pullman cars each night, attended by ineffably polite Black porters. All was not well with the 'world's greatest hotel', however, and George Pullman's rail-born empire slowly came off its tracks. Visionary inventor, brilliant businessman and high-minded social engineer though he was, Pullman was also stingy, monopolistic and racially biased. (Pullman Porters were always Black, but their traditional supervisors, the Pullman Conductors, were invariably White.) The public took aim at the company after the Pullman Strike of 1894 that killed 12 workers. Eventually, the Pullman Company was divested of its model 'company-town' south of Chicago, its railway car building division (Pullman-Standard) and its sleeping cars, which were sold to the railroads in 1968. The last Pullman-Standard-built sleeping car was Amtrak Superliner No. 32009, fittingly named *George M. Pullman*.

The next morning, I awoke to the aroma of fresh coffee coming from the dining car. The late actor and epicure Vincent Price wrote in his cookbook, *A Treasury of Great Recipes*, that the greatest breakfast he could remember was on a railroad dining car. Amtrak no longer makes the puffy French toast that was Price's favourite, but my simple eggs-and-sausage breakfast was hard to beat as I watched the sunrise over the Great Plains in the east, while the moon set behind the Rocky Mountains in the west.

The California Zephyr rolled to a stop at the stately Beau Arts-style Denver Union Station to refuel for the stupendous climb up the Front Range of the Rockies, through Moffat Tunnel and down via the canyon lands to Salt Lake City, Utah – the most scenic railway trip in America.

No railroad builder had more vision and determination, nor was more admired than Denver's favourite son, David H. Moffat. Denver

The Machu Picchu Vistadome

CUSCO TO AGUAS CALIENTES, PERU

BY TOM SAVIO

ROUTE *Cusco–Aguas Calientes station (Machu Picchu), Peru, South America.* **DISTANCE** *110km (68 miles).*
DURATION *Approximately 3 hours and 15 minutes.* **GAUGE** *914mm (3ft).*

The story of the railway to Machu Picchu is both ancient and modern. It began in the 15th century, when the Inca built a city atop Machu Picchu (Old Mountain), 400m (1312ft) above the Rio Urubamba. However, the flanged-wheel-on-steel-rail perspective of the story had its origins in 1905, when the Peruvian government proposed the 914mm (3ft) gauge Cusco–Santa Ana Railway. The route was projected 193km (120 miles) northwest from Cusco through the valley of the Rio Urubamba to the riches of coffee and tropical fruits in the Santa Ana region beyond Machu Picchu.

In the exuberance of the railway-building age many routes were proposed, fewer were built and even less reached their intended destinations. So it was with the ambitious Cusco–Santa Ana line. Construction was delayed until 1921; it never reached its intended terminus and probably never will, after a devastating landslide severed the line beyond Aguas Calientes, at the foot of Machu Picchu.

Until the 20th century only the local Quechua villagers knew the location of Machu Picchu. Abandoned by the Inca after the Spanish conquest of Peru, it remained unknown to the outside world until archaeologist Hiram Bingham rediscovered it in 1911. Then, in 1948, Bingham personally opened a twisting gravel road from Aguas Calientes to the Machu Picchu ruins, and the destinies of the railway and Machu Picchu became permanently entwined. The ruins, designated a UNESCO World Heritage Site in 1985, can be reached only by a 3¼-hour train ride, or by a strenuous three-to-five day trek along the ancient Inca Trail.

When I flew into Cusco to ride the railway, I travelled from sea level up to 3352m (11,000 ft), and 200 years back in time. Cusco is an unspoilt city of Spanish Colonial Baroque architecture resting on ancient foundations of precise Inca masonry. Hidden amid its cobblestone warrens is The Monasterio Hotel. Originally a monastery built in 1595 after the Spanish conquest of the Inca capital, it is now the favoured base for railway trekkers. Among its colonnaded gardens, gilded chapel and sumptuous 17th-century ecclesiastical paintings, railway wanderers from around the world feast on roast alpaca and try to acclimatize to the high altitude in oxygen-enriched suites.

If there is a heaven, I mused, it probably looks like The Monasterio, and its exquisitely polite staff would be the angels. The hotel is managed by Orient-Express Hotels, operators of the Venice Simplon-Orient-Express, which came to Peru in 1999 to enhance its hospitality port-folio. Chairman James Sherwood studied the Peruvian government's new railway privatization tenders and other offers to operate The Monasterio and the Machu Picchu Sanctuary Lodge, the only hotel at the ruins. The concept seemed ideal – a scenic railway linking two World Heritage sites – anchored by unique hotels. But after a first-hand inspection of the properties and the ramshackle railway, the concept lost its lustre. Then Simon Sherwood – James's son and scion of the mansion Orient-Express – recalling his youthful rambles along the Inca Trail, interceded on behalf of Peru's railway and hotel heritage. Consequently, a partnership was formed with Peru Hotels, S.A., and a 30-year railway concession was acquired with Peruval Corp.

New rail and ballast was laid, rolling stock renovated, the right-of-way tidied and the railway was reborn as PeruRail. Today, with much work yet to be done, General Manager Yasmine Martin and her Peruvian staff operate the Machu Picchu Vistadome train with the care and precision of the Glacier Express in her native Switzerland. It's called the Vistadome because the Spanish-built 'autowagons' (self-propelled diesel railcars) sport panoramic windows front, side and overhead.

LEFT *In this famous and unique vista, the Machu Picchu Vistadome comes into view through the El Arco aqueduct as it makes its way from Cusco to Aguas Calientes.*

The Vistadome followed the roaring Rio Urubamba through the Sacred Valley of the Inca. Ancient temples and terraces cascaded down the mountains on both sides. At Ollantaytambo we rolled to a stop and were surrounded by native vendors offering rugs, dolls and prized *chuclo* corn through the open windows of the train. Then a railway policeman rang a large bronze bell – the 'all aboard' in South America – and the vendors pulled back as we rumbled out of town.

Ahead lay the deep, dark green Urubamba Gorge and the cloud forest, habitat of wild orchids, giant hummingbirds and the endangered

LEFT *A Quechuan woman in traditional dress marks time for a local train as the Vistadome rolls past the Pachar depot in the Sacred Valley of the Inca.*
BELOW *Hard on the tail lights of the deluxe Vistadome, a standard-class 'Backpacker' train calls at the Ollantaytambo station amid a sea of local vendors hawking fresh corn, folk art, blankets and native dolls.*

ABOVE *The central area of Machu Picchu with the Temple of the Sun in the centre foreground and the summit of Huayna Picchu.*

speckled bear. The smooth dark walls of the gorge folded over the line like pumpernickel dough, which the railway pierced with nine short tunnels. Some were so inexplicably short that they resembled the old-fashioned papier-mâché tunnels on model railways. Expatriate American con man and Peruvian railway magnifico, 'Don Enrique' Meiggs, believed that a proper railway needed at least one tunnel, even if a few sticks of cheap dynamite could easily clear the obstinate mountain from the right-of-way. Meiggs was long gone when this railway was built, but apparently his spirit had a hand in its construction.

Beyond the tunnels, the jungle-covered mountains took on the pointed profiles that are familiar to all who have seen a travel poster of Machu Picchu. At Aguas Calientes, the passengers surged through the station concourse and down the long cobblestone street, past the souvenir hawkers in the *mercado* (market) to the jitney buses to Machu Picchu. Photographs of Machu Picchu – a ruined city clinging to a sheer mountaintop in the jungle mists – have become icons of popular culture. Yet pictures cannot convey the scale of the ruins. The crowds nearly vanished among the houses, temples and palaces; visitors appeared like specks on the grassy boulevard to Huayna Picchu (Young Mountain), the peak that dominates the view.

On a precipice high above the Urubamba, native workers straddled the beam of a restored hut while nonchalantly thatching its roof, much as their ancestors might have done 500 years before. The weather alternated from hot and sunny to cool, damp and dreary as clouds and mist drifted by, enhancing Machu Picchu's deeply mystical aura – a Pompeii in the sky.

EUROPE

LEFT *The Bernina Railway on the spiral at Brusio.*

The West Highland Line

BY ANTHONY LAMBERT

ROUTE *Glasgow–Mallaig, Scotland.* **DISTANCE** *264km (164 miles).*
DURATION *5 hours 13 minutes one way.* **GAUGE** *1435mm (4ft 8¹/₂ in).*

'A line for All Seasons.' The Jacobite. The title of a marketing campaign and the name of the summer steam-hauled trains that operate between Fort William and Mallaig encapsulate the great appeal of the West Highland Line. The landscape, shaped on a majestic scale, deserves to be seen at varying times of the year, but when pressed, local railwaymen favour a clear winter's day. And the country through which the line passes is redolent with the tragic story behind the final withering of the Stuart cause.

A smidgen under 160km (100 miles), the Fort William section of the West Highland Line begins at Craigendoran Junction on the suburban route between Glasgow and Helensburgh. It was one of the last railways to be built in Britain, opening to Fort William in 1894; the 67km (42 miles) to Mallaig opened in 1901. Financial assistance from the government reflected its purpose in stimulating economic development in a desolate region, and the railway's original directors included local landowners such as the euphoniously titled Cameron of Lochiel and Mackintosh of Mackintosh.

Single track throughout, with passing loops at most stations, the line was built with economy, avoiding tunnelling (there are only two before Fort William) and accepting prolonged gradients as stiff as 1 in 54. Although privatization has fragmented almost familial relationships,

this is the kind of line where the staff still care enough to advise their passengers when they have time to stretch their legs at stations if the train is waiting to cross (meet) an oncoming service.

Our trip begins at Glasgow Queen Street Station, gazing out of the window of an uninspiring diesel multiple unit at the impressive overall roof. The 1 in 42 climb out of Queen Street is so steep that trains were cable-hauled until locomotives became powerful enough. On the west side, at the top of the bank, once stood Cowlairs works, where many of the locomotives and carriages that ran over the West Highland were built.

The flanges squeal on the check-railed curve to Cowlairs North Junction, pointing the train in a westerly direction for the run through the western suburbs. The occasional belt of trees is a welcome screen to the acres of soulless distribution centres and unimaginative housing developments. Past Westerton the line burrows underneath the Forth & Clyde Canal, which in 1803 witnessed the first commercial application of steam power to waterborne traffic.

Singer Station takes its name from the well-known American sewing-machine company, which set up a factory here in 1883. The first hills come into view to the north-west, while to the south lies the Erskine suspension bridge that carries the A898 across the Clyde; this cable-stayed, box-girder bridge was built in 1967–71 by Freeman Fox

LEFT Shortly after leaving Fort William, on the line from Fort William to Mallaig, this steam train is dwarfed by the hulk of Ben Nevis, the highest mountain in the United Kingdom.

treeless peat bogs, with the occasional pickled tree roots to remind onlookers that, long ago, the area was part of the great Caledonian Forest. Beside Rannoch station is a cluster of buildings created solely for the few railwaymen required here as signalman, lengthman and station staff. At the northern end is an effigy of J.H. Renton, carved by the navvies in appreciation of the way he devoted part of his fortune to saving the line when it was threatened with bankruptcy during its construction in 1894.

It was at Rannoch, in 1894–5, long before global warming put paid to seriously harsh winters, that members of the Fort William Curling Club were stranded when their train became stuck fast. By the time snowplough locomotives fought their way through the drifts, they were in a poor way through lack of food. It is not unusual for a couple of dozen walkers to get on at Rannoch, providing more custom today than at any time since 1894.

Beyond the viaduct curving east, north of the station, the train burrows through the avalanche shed at Cruach, built to protect a cutting particularly vulnerable to snow drifts, and the only such shelter on Britain's railways. You would be unlucky not to see a stag during the crossing of the moor, especially in winter, though the colour of the animals' coats camouflages them well against the russet landscape. Corrour station, the highest on the line, is confirmation of the importance of walkers to the local economy; the adjacent station house has been converted into a restaurant and well-appointed bunkhouse. Children at remote stations and railway cottages once received a pre-Christmas visitation from a white-bearded man in a red cloak bearing gifts, brought by a special locomotive and brake van.

RIGHT *Class 37 No. 37425 heads a Fort William to London sleeping car train between Bridge of Orchy and Tyndrum, Ben Doran looming behind.*
BELOW *The 21-arch, 380m (416yd) long Glenfinnan Viaduct conveys the line between the two flanks of the Glenfinnan.*

Westward across Ireland

DUBLIN TO TRALEE, IRELAND

BY DAVID LAWRENCE

ROUTE *Dublin–Tralee in County Kerry, Ireland.* **DISTANCE** *332km (206 miles).*
DURATION *about 4¹/₂ hours.* **GAUGE** *1600mm (5ft 3in).*

Ireland cannot offer lines through spectacular mountain passes or luxury trains with sumptuous meals, but it does offer unique Irish scenery and folk as hospitable as one can meet. Thus my nomination for a journey is simply to buy an ordinary (or a rover or Domino) ticket and use one of the two daily through trains from Heuston Station in Dublin to Tralee in County Kerry. This is a journey of 332km (206 miles), and the longest ride possible in the country without a change.

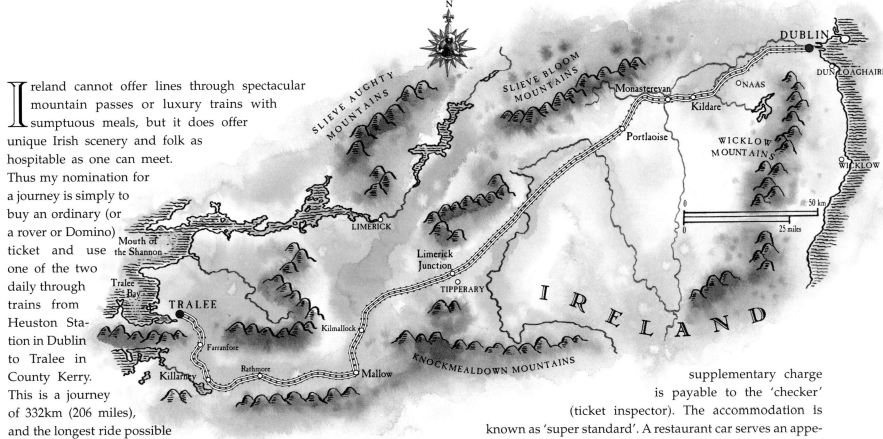

Our ride is mainly over the 1600mm (5ft 3in) double-track main line from Dublin to Cork (the only other substantial double line is to Belfast), but we branch off at Mallow onto a simple secondary route, through world-famous Killarney, that still retains old semaphore signals with sleepy wayside stations – some now closed.

After Ireland (or at least that part then known as the Irish Free State) broke away from the United Kingdom in 1922, Dublin developed its new status as a capital, and is now restoring its wealth of Georgian architecture. Among the grandest of its structures is Heuston Station, a classical, mainly unaltered building designed by English architect Sancton Wood, and opened in 1845. The station is close to the River Liffey, over a mile upstream, and is thus a long but pleasant walk, bus or taxi ride from town along the former quays.

The through trains to Tralee leave at around 08:30 and 18:30. Other timings are possible by changing at Mallow, and timetables (as in Britain) differ on Sundays. Carriages are comfortable with a small area of first class (at the Tralee end of the train), for which a flat

LEFT *On a beautifully clear and sunny day, an Irish Rail Class 201 diesel-electric arrives at Kildare in County Kerry on its 332km (206-mile) journey from Dublin to Tralee.*

supplementary charge is payable to the 'checker' (ticket inspector). The accommodation is known as 'super standard'. A restaurant car serves an appetizing range of snacks, and full meals in the form of well-prepared grills; super standard passengers are waited upon at their seats.

Speeds are not more than 160kph (100 mph), so it is pleasant to watch the passing scene on a journey of around 4½ hours each way. Railways in Britain and Ireland are still measured in miles, and the Great Southern & Western Railway, which built the Cork main line and most of its branches, erected huge stone mileposts at every quarter mile from Dublin. Further south, they are made of metal. These measurements are easy to read and can thus be used to identify points of interest en route. (I use east and west for simplicity although the line is essentially from north-east to south-west as far as Mallow, and runs westwards from there.) The mileage begins at zero at Heuston Station and reaches 144½ by Mallow, where they start again for the branch, reaching 61½ at Tralee.

We climb out of Dublin, usually with one of Irish Rail's largest diesel locomotives at the head. These Canadian-built General Motors 201-class machines are named after Irish rivers; nameplates are above the cab window – in English on one side and in Gaelic on the other.

At around 17½ miles, just before Sallins, the Grand Canal will be glimpsed at its junction for the cut to the Shannon River and branch to Naas and Corbally. At one time, Irish canals were very busy with freight but for around 40 years they have had a quieter time with leisure boats in summer. We see the canal again at Monasterevan

Norwegian Railways to the Arctic Circle

OSLO TO BODØ, NORWAY

BY ANTHONY LAMBERT

ROUTE *Oslo–Bodø, Norway.* **DISTANCE** *1282km (797 miles).*
DURATION *2 days (one way), with a stopover in Trondheim.* **GAUGE** *1435mm (4ft 8¹/₂in).*

Railway construction in Europe was generally a swift affair, proceeding as rapidly as the technological means of the day would allow. But the railway that links the Norwegian capital with Bodø, beyond the Arctic Circle, took an astonishing 108 years to complete, linking the very beginnings of railways with the modern era. The first section was engineered by the English pioneer of steam locomotives, Robert Stephenson, and a diesel-hauled train formally opened the final section in 1962.

The journey is further than the distance from Oslo to northern Italy, so it is not surprising that the 1282km (797-mile) line is operated in two sections, from Oslo to Trondheim, and from there to Bodø. A day is required for each, and visitors may want to break the trip by spending at least a day in Trondheim, once Norway's capital and then known as Nidaros. Norwegian State Railways operates Oslo–Trondheim with its *Signatur* tilt trains, which are among Europe's most thoughtfully designed and comfortable, while those to Bodø are diesel-hauled stock.

The journey begins at Oslo Sentral, its 1877–82 façade and entrance hall masking the rebuilt and extended station beyond. The first part of the journey is over the high-speed railway to Gardermoen Airport and Eidsvoll, through gently rolling hills with pleasant woods of conifer and birch breaking up the farmland. At Eidsvoll, the old line built by Stephenson and opened in his presence in 1854 trails in from the east. Following the

River Vorma, the railway reaches the southern end of Norway's largest lake, Mjøsa, on which you may be able to enjoy the sight of the world's oldest working paddlesteamer, the *Skibladner*, which was built in 1856 and still plies the lake during the warmer months.

After a long stretch beside the lake, the railway climbs away from the shore to give panoramic views over a seemingly endless succession of hills in all directions. The vast majority of farm buildings are painted an identical shade of crimson brown, as though responding to a state diktat issued by a Henry Ford of agrarian buildings. By the time you reach the important railway workshop town of Hamar, the line has returned to the lakeside. It runs all the way along it to the northern end of the lake at Lillehammer, famous for hosting the 1994 Winter Olympics.

Birch and conifers cover the steep slopes of Gudbrandsdal, which the train follows all the way to Dombås. Farming and forestry occupy most of the communities, supplemented by an occasional quarry and tourism based on skiing and walking near Vinstra. As the train presses north, more of the farm buildings sport overlapping corners, bringing to mind similar construction methods in northern Canada, which this countryside increasingly resembles.

After hanging above an impressive gorge on the east of the valley, the train climbs towards the junction at Dombås so that the Trondheim line can climb out of Gudbrandsdal and turn northeast over the mountain plateau. Some passengers leave the train here to catch the connecting scenic Rauma railway down to Andalsnes at the head of Romsdalfjord. To escape the valley, Trondheim trains describe a semi-circle onto a bleak upland punctuated by few trees and barely a sign of habitation, with a backdrop of snow-covered peaks. In winter, cross-country skiers with their long slender skis detrain at the isolated and well-shuttered station of Hjerkinn. Passing the area's highest mountain, the 2286m (7500ft)

LEFT Trondheim station, here covered in snow, is isolated from the town by an inlet of the River Nidelva. Various interesting sights in the old quarter of the town are all within easy walking distance of the station.

Le Petit Train Jaune

PERPIGNAN TO TOULOUSE, FRANCE

BY ANTHONY LAMBERT

ROUTE *Perpignan–Ile-sur-Têt–Vinça–Villefranche–Thuès Carança–Fontpédrouse-St-Thomas-les-Bains–Mont-Louis-la-Cabanasse–Bolquere-Eyne–Bourg-Madame– La-Tour-de-Carol–L'Hospital-près-L'Andorre–Ax-les-Thermes–Tarascon-sur-Ariège–Toulouse; French Pyrenees.* **DISTANCE** *272km (169 miles).* **DURATION** *7 hours.* **GAUGE** *1m (3ft 3¹/₂in) and 1435mm (4ft 8¹/₂in).*

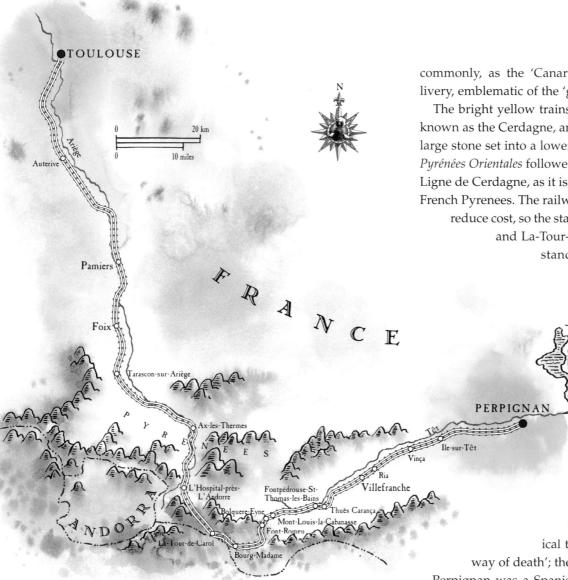

commonly, as the 'Canary' because of its unusual yellow-and-red livery, emblematic of the 'gold and blood' colours of Catalonia.

The bright yellow trains run through an area of the high Pyrenees known as the Cerdagne, and characteristic of the stations en route is a large stone set into a lower course of the building and engraved with *Pyrénées Orientales* followed by the altitude. The plateau served by the Ligne de Cerdagne, as it is officially known, is the sunniest area of the French Pyrenees. The railway was built to metre gauge (3ft 3 3/8in) to reduce cost, so the stations at each end – Villefranche-de-Conflent and La-Tour-de-Carol – are interchange points with the standard gauge lines from Perpignan and Toulouse respectively.

Even before the first section opened, between Villefranche and Mont-Louis in July 1910, the Cerdagne railway had received publicity of a most unwanted kind: during the formal inspection of the Gisclard bridge in 1909, the train carrying the official party hurtled off the track near the bridge. Engineer Albert Gisclard himself and five others were killed, due, the inquiry revealed, to a defect in the brake system compounded by human error. The media were as hysterical then as now, and branded the line 'the railway of death'; the railway has operated safely ever since.

Perpignan was a Spanish possession for over two hundred years until 1642, and the palm-shaded streets have a strong Mediterranean air. Railways were a popular subject of 19th-century French artists in particular, but Perpignan station was dubbed by Salvador Dalí 'the centre of the world', an absurdity commemorated in a stone above an arch near the entrance which reads 'Centre du Monde: 0.0km'. Trains for Villefranche turn west almost immediately after leaving the station, crossing the River Basse as it threads through the city centre, and head towards the Têt valley.

As the train leaves the city and passes through an area of polytunnels and open market gardening, the Mediterranean flavour extends to the rural housing, the roofs covered with terracotta pantiles and the rendered walls painted a pale pink-brown. To the south the foothills of the nearby range rise up from the coastal plain, while beyond a higher range already bears a crown of snow. Cypress and poplars

The Pyrenees, second only to the Alps for the difficult terrain they presented to European railway builders, stretch for 435km (270 miles) and provide a vast natural barrier between France and Spain. The only two major railway arteries that link these two countries hug the coast at each end of the mountain chain. The most fascinating of the two secondary routes that weave through the higher areas runs between the coast at Perpignan and Toulouse via one of France's most intriguing narrow gauge railways. It is known either as *Le Petit Train Jaune* (The Little Yellow Train), or, less

LEFT *Mont-Louis-la-Cabanasse is one of the busiest stations on the narrow gauge section of The Little Yellow Train, because of the tourist appeal of the fortified town it serves.*

The Venice Simplon-Orient-Express

PARIS TO ISTANBUL, ACROSS EUROPE

BY TOM SAVIO

ROUTE *Paris–Budapest–Bucharest–Varna–Istanbul.* **DISTANCE** *3718km (2310 miles).*
DURATION *6 days, 5 nights (one way).* **GAUGE** *1435mm (4ft 8½in).*

The most celebrated train in the pantheon of legendary travel was an elite caravan of cultivated carriages called the *Orient-Express*. History has crowned it 'King of Trains and Train of Kings' for its luxurious appointments and anointed clientele. Like most great works of art it was the creation of one man, the Belgian engineer Georges Nagelmackers.

While touring America in 1869, Nagelmackers was very impressed by the Pullman Palace Car Company's luxurious sleeping-car service that rolled seamlessly over a patchwork of railroads spanning the vast country, and imagined a similar network of posh trains knitting together Europe's jumble of kingdoms, principalities, sultanates and republics. Upon his return to Belgium he soon organized the *Compagnie Internationale des Wagons-Lits* (International Sleeping Car Company), or 'Madame la Compagnie' to the cognoscenti, and readied plans to bridge the breadth of the continent with the most glamourous train the world had ever seen. On 4 October 1883, Wagons-Lits launched its first railway passenger service linking Paris with Constantinople (now Istanbul), Turkey. It was eventually and fortuitously dubbed the Orient-Express.

To expedite the 3058km (1900-mile) journey across Europe's borders, Wagons-Lits and the respective governments signed *ententes cordiales*, ensuring that customs and immigration formalities would now be conducted on board the train for the first time, so that fashionable passengers were not unnecessarily incommoded, or the train delayed. Although speed was a hallmark of the Orient-Express, it earned its coveted cachet for its lavish carriages, fabled service and the

pedigree of its passenger lists. Kings, queens, maharajahs and impresarios all held court in its palatial carriages, feasting on lobster, truffles and champagne, while diplomats, spies, arms merchants and courtesans discreetly pursued their intrigues. Mata Hari rode the Orient-Express to her German rendezvous, and King Boris of Bulgaria often drove the train's engine across his realm.

Not surprisingly, many literary and theatrical works were inspired by the train's long and storied run, and some were surprisingly close to the truth. The most celebrated of these was undoubtedly the Agatha Christie mystery *Murder on the Orient Express*, and its subsequent Sidney Lumet film adaptation. In both book and film, the crime was committed when the train was snowbound in Eastern Europe.

In reality, the Orient-Express was snowbound near the Turkish town of Çerkesköy during the calamitous winter of 1929. Murder, however, was not on the menu – nor was anything else for that matter, because the restaurant-car pantry was emptied during the six-day ordeal. When the starving passengers finally tunnelled out of the train, they confronted the armed villagers of a nearby hamlet who

LEFT *Nyugati Station in Budapest – one of the proud monuments that attest to the intrepid genius of the French structural engineer whose most famous creation is the Eiffel Tower in Paris.*

ABOVE *The Orient-Express features the ultimate in luxury interiors. Here, priceless Lalique glass panels are seductively lit by a dainty side lamp.*

were jealously guarding their surplus provisions. It was a rather tense standoff until the townsfolk were persuaded to trade their goods, practically weight for weight, for the passenger's gold coins.

For over 90 years the Orient-Express survived, in spite of two world wars, a worldwide depression and the anxieties of the Cold War. But it could not be reconciled with the postwar appetite for motorways and mediocrity. No train in history ever eclipsed the aura that radiated from the Orient-Express. It was dimmed only by the shadow of the jet plane. After years of decline, the tattered train made its last run to Istanbul on 19 May 1977.

I was smitten with the legend of the Orient-Express while watching the famous Sidney Lumet movie starring Albert Finney and a galaxy of screen legends in outrageously campy cameo roles. I was mesmerized when the carriage doors slammed shut, the whistle

screeched and the camera moved slowly in on the locomotive's darkened headlamp, which suddenly filled the screen with brilliant light as the Orient-Express glided away, consigned, seemingly forever, to a bygone time.

American James B. Sherwood is a visionary bon vivant and global hotel, railway and shipping magnate. Having grown weary of the anonymous business hotels he frequented as the president of Sea Containers Group, Sherwood acquired his own family of exquisite hostelries that were convenient to the ports served by his firm. To these holdings, he impulsively added two vintage Orient-Express carriages from a now-legendary Monte Carlo auction. Eventually the two grew to a fleet of 30, with siblings from other prestigious trains, including the British Pullman Company's *Brighton Belle* and Wagons-Lits' *Train Bleu*. Their exquisite Albert Dunn marquetry, chinoise lacquer walls, René Prou Art Deco inlays and René Lalique glass panels were lovingly restored by some of the families and firms that had originally designed and furnished them.

The magnificent carriages evolved into two distinct touring trains. The British Pullman, liveried in umber and cream, would run from Sherwood's London base to the English Channel. The Continental Train, in Wagons-Lits blue and cream, would take over from the French coast to Paris, then via the Simplon Tunnel to Venice and Sherwood's Cipriani Hotel. The channel crossing itself was to be by ferry (later by Eurotunnel's Le Shuttle train). On 25 May 1982, the Venice Simplon-Orient-Express donned the mantle of its illustrious predecessor – with the blessings of 'Madame la Compagnie' – and 'the world's most celebrated train' was reborn.

For over 20 years, the VSOE's seasonal sojourns evolved with varying routes and destinations. Perennial favourite, however, is the re-creation of the Orient-Express run from Paris to Istanbul. In its heyday, there were several Orient-Express trains on different routes. The VSOE generally follows the itinerary of the Arlberg-Orient-Express. Only one train is programmed each year because of the complexity of integrating the VSOE's unique schedule with the normal flow of rail traffic in France, Switzerland, Liechtenstein, Austria, Germany, Hungary, Romania, Bulgaria and Turkey. International celebrities, honeymoon couples, railway romantics, mystery fans, and those who were simply 'born too late' book well in advance to assure their berths onboard VSOE's 'magic carpet to the East'.

Paris was sunny and peaceful in August. Most Parisians seemed to be away on holiday, and those who had stayed in the city were relaxed and friendly to visitors. But the weather turned sultry, and it began to rain when I boarded the polished carriages of the Venice Simplon-Orient-Express in the Gare de l'Est. In my sleeping car compartment, among the stationery, souvenirs and chocolates was a hand fan. The VSOE excels in subtleties, and this was a gentle reminder that we were travelling to Istanbul in the summer, and the train was not air-conditioned.

From its blue-and-cream livery to the burnished bronze letters that spell out the splendidly complete appellation *Compagnie Internationale des Wagons-Lits et des Grands Express Européens*, the VSOE is of two worlds. Although it is Mr Sherwood's fabulous rolling hotel, the name *Orient-Express* and the Wagons-Lits' iconography are the property of Madame la Compagnie. VSOE uses them with the stipulation that the Continental carriages are to be maintained in their historic configurations to the degree that safety and reason permit. Indeed, the French Ministry of Culture lists a small fleet of similar carriages still owned by Wagons-Lits as national monuments. Consequently, the décor, coke-fired heaters, hand-cranked windows and quaint end-of-hall brass-levered toilets have been retained. The carriages are innocent of en-suite facilities, showers and air conditioning. The VSOE is a virtual time machine: passengers experience all the luxury (and some of the inconveniences) of journeying during the *belle époque* of rail travel – the Roaring Twenties – when the carriages were built.

Over a dinner of sea bass and caviar I met my fellow travellers. There was an American mining heiress and Elizabeth Taylor look-alike. She possessed the kind of self-assured presence that blesses the very rich. Then there was a Canadian railfan who expounded the history along the line. Across the aisle sat a very suntanned 70ish American who introduced himself as 'the biggest highway builder in Texas', and his vivacious Latina bride. Sharing my table was a Catalonian war correspondent and his sociologist wife. He had just returned from the Balkans and was keeping his bags packed for the Middle East. She delighted in taking 'clinical notes' during the voyage, and by the end of the journey could sort out who among her 'subjects' had rendezvoused with whom. We all dined and talked till midnight.

It was a warm drizzly summer night, so I threw off the blankets, cranked open the window and kept the fan close at hand. Sleep came easily, as it always does for me on a train. I'm where I always want to be, on the railway going anywhere. The occasional crescendo of passing freight trains only reassured me that the railway was earning

ABOVE *Some things never change: exclusive service still awaits passengers on the Venice Simplon-Orient-Express and friendly staff welcome the guests aboard.*

money. Later, I was startled awake by a frigid wind blowing into my cabin – the gentle French drizzle had turned to snow in Switzerland. I cranked shut the window, wrapped myself in all the bedclothes and stored the hand fan under the bunk, where it remained unused for the remainder of the trip. Piero, my buoyant Venetian cabin steward, had his hands very full, frantically stoking the car heater, answering calls from passengers for more blankets and preparing the hearty Continental breakfasts.

If I can find any fault at all with overnight European train travel, including even the VSOE, it is the high-fat, high-sugar, low-protein Continental breakfast that is served in the morning – and when we stopped in Linz, Austria, to water the train, I vanished into the station bistro. The Baroness, my wife, is Austrian, so I knew that a hearty breakfast was at hand. My broiled ham and eggs arrived on vintage Compagnie des Wagons-Lits porcelain. I could barely contain myself, as this was the very pattern needed to complete my dining-car crockery collection. I asked Herr Ober what I owed for the meal and the plate on which it was served, and mentioned my wife's ancestry. Amused, he wrapped the booty, charged for the meal alone, and waved-off my substantial 'tip'.

Although the VSOE is the Continent's most prestigious train, we were obliged to wait for Austria's top train, the Transalpin. To make up for lost time, the VSOE scurried down the new high-speed bypass line, away from the scenic Danube river route and through a long tunnel that exited next to a McDonald's hamburger emporium. I felt as though the train had burrowed beneath the ocean to the USA instead of the bluffs along the Danube. We made a long loop, avoiding Vienna, and raced across the Hungarian frontier, arriving to the thunderous chords of the Fire Brigade Band and crowds of curious commuters in Budapest's Nyugati Station. The lacy ironwork has Parisian flair, since it was designed in 1874 by Alexandre Gustave

Eiffel, the engineer who built the Parisian icon and many graceful railway structures from Budapest to Portugal and Peru.

The Hungarians, with their warm and unaffected old-world charm, are definitely among my favourite Europeans. The passengers transferred to the Marriott Hotel for showers and stationary beds, but I boarded a vintage railbus that shuttles between the station and the Hungarian Railway History Park, where I renewed some old friendships and got the railway 'skinny' on the next day's big event.

The following morning, while most of the passengers were out sightseeing in Budapest or enjoying lunch at Grundel's, the VSOE rolled into the Railway Park for a presentation honouring the new museum. The eminent backdrop for this affair, and proud centrepiece of the collection, was the Hungarian teak-and-bronze dining car No. 2347 that had formerly been assigned to the Orient-Express in 1912.

We dined across the Great Hungarian Plain that evening and crossed into Romania. In the morning, while climbing through Carpathian Mountains, the Canadian fan spotted a chuffing steam locomotive working in a factory yard, confirming my sense that I was travelling back in time. Our next destination was the Romanian mountain resort of Sinaia, where we retraced the steps of the very first Orient-Express passengers who had dined here in Peles Castle. King Carol, who was excited at prospects of the Orient-Express opening Romania

ABOVE *Towering slopes clad in fairytale forests, and bridges spanning waterfalls gushing off the mountainsides characterize the Austrian stretch of the journey.*

to the west, hosted a gala dinner for its pioneering passengers in his charmingly ostentatious, half-timbered and turreted 116-room 'hunting lodge' in the mountains above town.

We exchanged the lush Carpathians for a dusty and dun-coloured landscape of mud-brick houses, bearded men in slouch hats and well-worn tweeds driving horse buggies. The verdant landscapes of Western Europe, framed by my cabin window, had evolved into a sepia-tone travelogue from the 1930s. In keeping with that era, we pulled into Bucharest's Stalinist-style Presidential Station, the private terminal of Romania's late tyrant, Nicolae Ceausescu, who, along with his wife Elena, was executed in 1989 during a violent revolution. We toured the Kafkaesque communist-era monuments and Ceausescu's rambling official residence, a contrast of rich Romanian folk mosaics and tasteless gold-plated fixtures. The cabinet chamber displayed Madame Ceausescu's enormous collection of matched shoes and purse sets that differed only in their pastel shades. The Ceausescus' possessions were practically all that remained of the national treasury, we were told, since after their fall the country's gold reserves had vanished. The kitschy ensembles were for sale to help restore the

residence, but no one wanted souvenirs of the appalling regime. A traditional Romanian banquet at the Athenee Palace Hotel, and the prospect of hot showers and roomy beds lifted our spirits that night.

Bulgaria is still ostensibly a communist state, but it was much gayer than newly democratic Romania. It had been the Soviet Union's staunchest ally and its espionage surrogate during the Cold War. And so I was surprised the next morning when the VSOE, a bourgeois icon during the Cold War, received its most enthusiastic welcome yet in the Bulgarian border town of Ruse. The platform was packed with well-wishers as well as the national media. Bouquets of fresh flowers were

BELOW *Today's Venice Simplon-Orient-Express retraces the route of the original Arlberg-Orient-Express over the viaducts and through the tunnels of the historic Arlberg Pass, above the idyllic Tyrolean town of Sankt Anton, Austria, on one of Europe's most scenic railway routes.*

The Golden Pass Route

LUZERN TO MONTREUX, SWITZERLAND

BY ANTHONY LAMBERT

ROUTE *Luzern–Sarnen–Meiringen–Interlaken–Spiez–Zweisimmen–Montreux, Switzerland.* **DISTANCE** *198km (123 miles).* **DURATION** *8 hours.*
GAUGE *metre gauge (3ft 3³/₈in) Luzern–Interlaken; 1435mm (4ft 8¹/₂in) Interlaken–Zweisimmen; metre gauge (3ft 3³/₈in) Zweisimmen–Montreux.*

The Golden Pass Route from Zürich to Geneva is a journey devised to give visitors to Switzerland an introduction to some of the country's finest landscapes, lakes and towns. It can be done in eight hours, but eight days would be better, stopping to savour some of the outstanding sights. The outer sections of the route, from Zürich to Luzern and from Montreux to Geneva, are by normal services, but the central three trains offer special coaches to give first-class passengers spectacular views and a special ambience.

From Luzern to Interlaken, the metre gauge (3ft 3⅜in) line is covered by panoramic coaches and a restaurant car. The line between Interlaken and Zweisimmen is operated by the standard gauge (1435mm; 4ft 8½in gauge) Bern–Lötschberg–Simplon Railway (BLS) with Salon Blue carriages. The last section is covered by the metre gauge Montreux–Oberland Bernois Railway (MOB), which has not only panoramic coaches but also driving trailers with glazed end windows allowing a view along the track ahead (or behind) while the driver sits in an elevated cab.

The terminus at Luzern stands right by the waters of the mountain-ringed lake that makes the city such a jewel. Close by is the steamer pier, still visited by the five magnificent paddlesteamers that share the timetable with modern motor vessels, and only a stone's throw away is Switzerland's most famous building, the Kapellbrücke (Chapel Bridge), across the River Reuss.

Not until the tunnel at Hergiswil are the suburbs of Luzern left behind. Beyond it lies the Alpnachersee, the far shore being a wall of immense cliffs rising up towards the summit of the Stanserhorn. The bright red cars on one of the world's steepest funiculars, up Mount Pilatus, can be seen as our train bowls through Alpnachstad station and heads for the capital of the forest canton of Obwalden at Sarnen. Leaving the station, the train hugs the eastern shore of Sarnensee to reach the start of the first rack section at Giswil, marked by a metallic clunk as each cog wheel engages the rack. Climbing steeply through thickening woodland, the train reaches the turquoise waters of

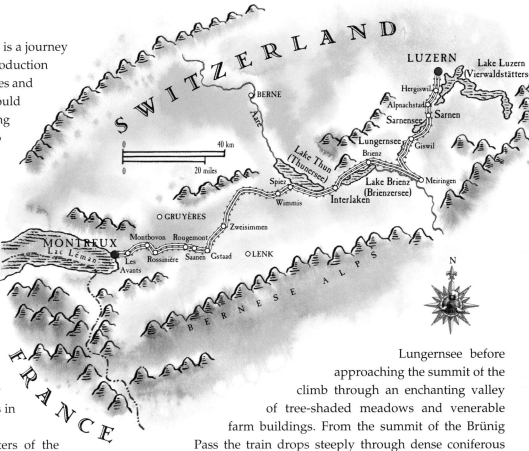

LEFT *The panoramic coaches on SBB's only metre gauge line, between Luzern and Interlaken, allow passengers to appreciate fully the spectacular landscape through which the line weaves its course.*

Lungernsee before approaching the summit of the climb through an enchanting valley of tree-shaded meadows and venerable farm buildings. From the summit of the Brünig Pass the train drops steeply through dense coniferous woods with occasional views over the broad valley of the Aare.

The rack section ends at Meiringen where the train has to reverse to head west towards Lake Brienz. Meiringen begat the meringue, and also has links with Sir Arthur Conan Doyle, who set the scene of Sherlock Holmes's death at the nearby Reichenbach Falls. The train makes the most of the flat, straight section to the eastern end of Lake Brienz, graced by the 1914 paddlesteamer *Lötschberg*. Steam of a different kind may be glimpsed at the woodcarvers' village of Brienz where the rack railway up Mount Rothorn starts, worked by steam locomotives dating from 1891 to 1996. The lake is never out of sight as the train makes for Interlaken, where many Golden Pass passengers make a detour to take the Jungfraubahn to Europe's highest railway station. Interlaken is built on the isthmus between Lake Brienz and Lake Thun, linked by the River Aare, which follows the railway through the trees to the north. The railway beyond the gateway to the Bernese Oberland is so picturesque that it once had double-deck carriages with longitudinal seats along the upper level for better views of the mountains around Lake Thun. The line is close to the water except where headlands stretch into the lake, sometimes creating a cove for a former fishing village such as Faulensee, prettily situated on a hill above an inlet.

ABOVE *A towering mountain dominates this Swiss landscape near Giswil.*
OPPOSITE *A Montreux–Oberland Bernois Railway train in the valley of the Saane, which can also be appreciated by balloon flights from Château d'Oex.*
BELOW *Luzern's historic Kapellbrücke (Chapel Bridge).*

By Spiez the line is high above the lake, and passengers have only a glimpse of the attractive harbour overlooked by the white-rendered castle with chevron-painted shutters and brightly tiled roofs. The train for Zweisimmen forks south west along the Simmental, renowned for its spectacularly decorated wooden chalets. At Wimmis the church and multi-roofed Schloss Weissenburg tower over the line as it forges up the narrow valley, its sides covered in woodland. If there is rivalry in Simmental, it must be over the profusion of one's window boxes that add vivid splashes of colour to the dark wood of the chalets.

As though to emphasize the woodworking skills of the valley, the junction station at Zweisimmen has attractive wooden canopies. Here the standard gauge terminates, but the metre gauge MOB offers the option of continuing south to Lenk, as well as the journey over its main line to Montreux. The sleek MOB train is appropriately known as the Crystal Panoramic Express and was designed by Pininfarina.

One of the delights of the MOB is that the train is at an almost continuously high level, affording magnificent views over one of the

loveliest parts of the country. The climb out of the Simmental begins the moment the train leaves Zweisimmen station, the train passing through pine woods and flower-strewn meadows before describing a loop through the Moosbach Tunnel and heaving itself over the shoulder of a hill into the valley of the Kleine (little) Simme. The summit of the line is reached at the small wintersports centre of Saanenmöser from where the line descends at gradients as steep as 1 in 25 to the famous resort of Gstaad, a jumble of chalet-style hotels at the confluence of several valleys.

The MOB takes the valley of the Saane to follow the river closely for much of the way to Montbovon. From Saanen speed picks up as the train encounters the first section of straight track, taking us to Rougemont, the first village in the French-speaking part of Switzerland, where the often rebuilt château is still protected by a multi-turreted curtain wall. Travelling along a shelf of rock with long drops down to the river, there are fantastic views over the pastoral valley and the mountains flanking the Rhône to the south. Hot-air balloons sometimes herald the approach to Château d'Oex, for this has become one of the world centres of the sport, made famous by Bertrand Picard and the *Breitling Orbiter*, which left earth at Château d'Oex on its round-the-world odyssey. The castle that gave its name to the town was burnt down in 1800, but the next village, Rossinière, has some of the largest and finest chalets in Canton Vaud, one with 113 windows and lavish decoration.

The valley narrows to a gorge before reaching Montbovon, junction for the line to Gruyères. The tunnel after Montbovon takes the train into a secluded well-wooded valley from where it climbs up towards Les Cases, squealing around a series of horseshoe bends. The straight, 2424m (2650yd) summit tunnel marks one of those dramatic transitions between not only very different landscapes but also weather systems; sun on one side can be replaced by misty cloud on the other.

The lonely station of Jor stands at the exit from the tunnel and it is soon evident why they used to take off and reattach dining cars here, for the line starts its dramatic descent through a series of horseshoe curves. But it is the astonishing view (on clear days) across Lac Léman towards the Dent-du-Midi in France that arrests everyone's attention. Dozens of white-capped peaks recede into the distance beyond Switzerland's largest lake. The line drops down through tunnels and woods past Les Avants, where Noël Coward lived from 1959 until his death in 1973, to Chamby, where weekend travellers may catch sight   a steam locomotive on the Blonay-Chamby line. Passing the stocky keep of the castle at Châtelard, the train approaches journey's end through a spiral tunnel into one of the world's few stations with three gauges.

Besides the metre and standard gauges, Montreux has the 800mm (2ft 7½in) gauge of the rack railway up Rochers-de-Naye, which has modern steam locomotives as well as electric trains. Though not one of Switzerland's most attractive towns, Montreux is famous for its festivals of jazz, classical music and television, and nearby is a building almost as well known as Luzern's Kapellbrücke, the lakeside castle immortalized by Byron's *The Prisoner of Chillon*.

The Bernina Railway

TIRANO TO ST MORITZ, SWITZERLAND

BY ANTHONY LAMBERT

ROUTE *Tirano, Italy, to St Moritz, Switzerland.* **DISTANCE** *61km (38 miles).*
DURATION *2 hours 20 minutes.* **GAUGE** *1m (3ft 3³/sin).*

The Alps offer weeks of spectacular railway journeys, so the accolade for top place must, inevitably, be a subjective choice. But the trains that link Tirano in Italy with one of Switzerland's most famous resorts, St Moritz, have a particular claim, for they climb over the highest rail crossing of the Alps, at 2256.5m (7403ft). Trains have to be lifted 1827m (5994ft) in 38.4km (24 miles) from Tirano to the summit at Ospizio Bernina. Moreover, they achieve this without recourse to the usual mechanical device of mountain-climbing railways, the rack and pinion. The trains of the Rhätische Bahn (RhB) spurn this costly contrivance and manage to ascend gradients of 1 in 14.3 relying purely on adhesion.

There is usually an optimum time of year to enjoy a railway journey, when nature is at its most impressive, but each season gives a very different aspect to the Bernina Railway and it is hard to make a preference. On a clear day of deep blue skies in mid-winter everything is mantled in snow, the waterfalls petrified and the trees weighed down with a mass of interlocking snowflakes much wider than the supporting branches. Before spring, the lower slopes are clear of snow and bleached the characteristic yellow-green of grass that has long been under snow. Switzerland is famous for its alpine flowers and the fresh greens of spring, while the warmth of summer encourages less hardy visitors to explore the higher regions. In autumn, the many deciduous trees turn the landscape into a veritable paintbox of oranges, yellows and browns.

Tirano is reached from Milan Central Station along a pleasant line that skirts Lake Como and heads up the long Valtellina to a terminus

LEFT *The most famous engineering feat on the picturesque Bernina Railway line is this spiral at Brusio, where the train passes through an arch of the curved viaduct to gain height.*

alongside that of the RhB. Palm trees used to grow in the town square, allowing the RhB to talk of Bernina trains taking you from the glaciers around St Moritz to palms in 2½ hours; they now have to be looked for in private gardens. Ordinary RhB trains have the advantage of windows that slide down, facilitating photography, but the air-conditioned panoramic coaches of the Bernina Express are supplemented for much of the year by open wagons with bench seats. Some of the all-stations stopping trains run as mixed trains, occasionally reversing at stations to drop off, or pick up, tanks of fuel, or wagons loaded with of timber or waste containers. An object lesson in efficiency, these operations are all carried out with minimal delay and never seem to cause a late arrival.

Trains leave Tirano through a yard that is often full of wagons laden with tree trunks, and turn north up the Poschiavo valley, gingerly crossing a square beside a church and forging up a street. Almost immediately the railway begins its sinuous climb, gaining altitude by hairpin bends through a succession of villages in the more populous lower end of the valley. Just before Brusio and its two tall campaniles, the railway spirals over itself by means of a nine-arch stone viaduct that circles three modern sculptures. The hazard of living in these valleys is illustrated by immense isolated rocks standing incongruously beside the railway or near housing – legacies of falls centuries ago.

From the station at Miralago, Lago di Poschiavo stretches northward towards the permanently snow-covered peaks surrounding the Bernina Pass. Along its western shore a path runs between the water and the railway while the eastern side is bordered for much of the way by a wall of rock rising hundreds of metres above the lake. Above are steeply forested slopes, broken only by the occasional fields of an

Alpine farm on precipitous slopes. After passing the curling rink beside the station at Le Prese, the train runs along the street with the river Poschiavino to the east.

With an hourly train service, it is easy to break the journey at Poschiavo to explore this architectural gem. Besides its many patrician houses with coats of arms encrusted on ancient stonework, the town has a Spanish quarter built by returning emigrants who had left their Italian-speaking home for Spain to work as hotel-keepers and pastry cooks. Continuing north from Poschiavo, the train begins the extraordinary climb by four horseshoe curves, some in spiral tunnels, that lift the line on the steepest section towards the summit. Curves are so

ABOVE *There are several sections of street running south of Poschiavo; this stretch is accompanied by much whistling – Swiss trains spurn the horn.*
RIGHT *The views from the steeply graded loops between Poschiavo and Cavaglia are some of the most spectacular to be had in Switzerland.*
BELOW *Lago di Poschiavo is skirted along its western shore by the railway line, as well as a cycle- and footpath.*

AFRICA

NAMIBIA
The Desert Express

SOUTH AFRICA
The Union Limited – Golden Thread

LEFT *The Desert Express in the barren Namib.*

The Desert Express

WINDHOEK TO SWAKOPMUND, NAMIBIA

BY ANTHONY LAMBERT

ROUTE *Windhoek–Swakopmund, Namibia.* **DISTANCE** *373km (232 miles).*
DURATION *About 20 hours (from 2pm to 10am the following day) one way.* **GAUGE** *1065mm (3ft 6in).*

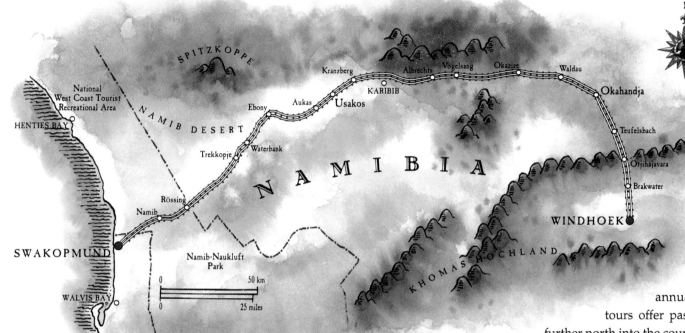

is a 373km (232-mile) journey between the capital, Windhoek, and the little coastal town Swakopmund. For many passengers, this short excursion will undoubtedly whet the appetite for more, and four-day journeys now form a regular part of the Desert Express's annual programme. These longer tours offer passengers the chance to venture further north into the country, to Tsumeb for a night at the four-star Mokuti Lodge on the edge of the Etosha National Park, or into the south to the Nest Hotel in Lüderitz, with a convenient visit to the abandoned diamond settlement of Kolmanskop.

The brilliant white station at Windhoek is an appropriately grand edifice for the departure of such a train. Built in 1912 and sympathetically extended twice, it is anachronistically large for the 12 ordinary departures each week plus two to three Desert Expresses, so its upper storey has become the TransNamib Railway Museum, which houses an astonishingly diverse collection of photographs and memorabilia.

When you have checked in, your bags are taken to your compartment and you have a chance to explore the train before departure. Most unusually, the carriages have asymmetrical hexagonal windows, and a bar/lounge car with a variety of comfortable seats adjoins the dining car. Books about Namibia, its flora and fauna, and the story of the railway are provided in the lounge car, and there is even a conference coach for meetings with a difference.

Once underway, a welcoming drink is an opportunity to meet the other passengers before the westbound journey stops, after less than an hour, at Otjihajavara Station where an open minibus meets the train and takes you to the nearby Okapuka ranch for lion-feeding time. The farm owners saved these cats when they became troublesome in a populous part of the country and were in danger of being shot. They now have the freedom of a spacious 35ha (87-acre) enclosure, and at tea time they receive a haunch of meat delivered on a wire-pulley system that encourages them to eat just feet away from the hide. Before returning to the train, a drink is provided in an open-sided building that overlooks lawns shaded by specimen trees before rocky soil and scrub take over.

If you have ever wondered why South West Africa was one of the very last parts of the continent to be colonized in the 'scramble for Africa', a journey on the Desert Express will answer that question. The country that became Namibia upon independence in 1990 is the driest south of the Sahara, with annual rainfall averaging a paltry 2.5cm (less than an inch), and it looks as unforgiving as these harsh statistics suggest. The landscape has an asperity that tells you life is a struggle, as well as a triumph of genetic adaptation, for almost every living thing in it.

Not for passengers on this train, though. The Desert Express was constructed in Namibia with German design input, and its eight luxurious passenger cars are designed to cocoon travellers from the heat and harshness outside. Although the track gauge is only 1065mm (3ft 6in) wide, the train's interior is as spacious as that of many standard gauge trains in Europe or the US; there is room for three berths (two transverse and one longitudinal) in each of the six ingeniously designed compartments per coach, as well as an en-suite shower, wash basin and lavatory. Much of the train is attractively panelled in pale woods, with liberal use of etched glass. Sound sleep is helped by individually controlled air-conditioning units, and the compartments convert to day use with cleverly collapsible armchairs. The usual itinerary

LEFT *As the sun rises, heralding yet another mercilessly hot day, the Desert Express makes its steady way through the African bush, while the engine driver surveys the passing scenery.*

ABOVE *The Desert Express en route to the cool relief of the coast.*
RIGHT *Quaint Windhoek Station – departure point for the journey through the Namib to the coastal town of Swakopmund.*

Despite the lack of rain, the leaves on the thorn trees visible from the line are an intense green in contrast to the seared brown of the ostrich grass of the bush. Oryx, warthog and giraffe may be seen, immune to the train's passing. The hills keep their distance on either side of the line, making it easier to spot game on the barely undulating plain.

Preprandial drinks are really sundowners, as the palette of blue, grey, red and orange deepens and changes by the moment. Dinner is cooked on board and is a credit to the two chefs: snails served on toast with a creamed spinach topping, or fresh Swakopmund asparagus with a Hollandaise sauce might be followed by smoked ostrich with green figs and a fresh salad, or a game-and-crumbled-maize medallion tower, complemented with a traditional brown sauce. In deference to many of the train's passengers, the piped music at dinner is mostly Beethoven, adding to the strong sense of German legacy, from rye bread to street names. This is all the more remarkable, for German occupation was short, from 1884 until 1915 when troops from the Union of South Africa accepted the surrender of the Imperial Governor after a campaign of almost a year.

Before 11pm, the train reaches the junction for the line north to Tsumeb at Kranzberg, where it halts for the night to allow passengers a restful sleep. Departure is soon after 4am and before dawn the train rolls through Usakos, where the principal railway workshops were located from 1904–5 until the early 1960s. At the western end of the town stands a large white church whose congregation would have consisted mostly of railwaymen.

At first light, it is apparent how different the passing landscape is from the previous day. Namibia is famous for its sands, most notably the Namib dune sea around Sossusvlei and Sesriem to the south, and sand covered by the stunted bush known as *Arthraerua leubnitziae* is all one sees until journey's end. The treeless desolation increases one's admiration for the pioneers in this country, whose ox-wagon journeys

from Windhoek to Swakopmund took at least three weeks; even the mail coach took 10 days.

It was little better for the *Schutztruppe* soldiers protecting the railway during World War I – a memorial to their privations can be seen beside the railway near Trekkopje, which you pass between dawn and breakfast. A stone coat of arms is a monument to the regimental mascot nicknamed 'Titbit', a goat accustomed to receiving titbits from the mess table, who returned the favour when rations of the bivouacked troops were near exhausted.

The Desert Express eases through the outlying township and the outskirts of Swakopmund while breakfast is being served and takes the line south to Walvis Bay, running parallel with the coast though the sea is out of sight beyond a high ridge of sand. At the passing loop

of Rand Rifles the train halts and the passengers are taken on a guided walk up to the top of the dunes for a view of the sea – on a clear day. All too often mist makes it impossible to tell you are looking down on the Atlantic Ocean and south towards what was once the tiny British, and subsequently South African, enclave and port of Walvis Bay, the country's only deepwater port. You quickly learn the secret of climbing sand dunes: by walking in the steps of the person in front you save most of the energy expended in compacting the sand for a foothold. What look like dark shadows on the dunes are areas of ilmenite, a black mineral composed of iron, titanium and oxygen that is mined in South Africa but not here in Namibia.

The strenuous dune walk over, the train returns to Swakopmund where there is plenty to occupy the visitor for several days. The town itself is a pleasure to explore, full of charming historic buildings such as the Woermann House of 1905, part of which is the Damara Tower, which offers a panorama of the town and coast from its belvedere. One can promenade along the seafront between avenues of thick-trunked palms, visit the Hansa Brauerei that has been slaking the country's thirst since 1929, or pay a visit to the Crystal Gallery, which displays various gemstones as well as the world's largest crystal cluster.

A further railway experience is offered at the best hotel in town that now occupies the former station building, a magnificent edifice of 1901 that has been carefully adapted and extended. The restaurant walls are decorated with railway memorabilia and photographs, some of them showing scenes on the route you have just taken, when the pampered comfort of the Desert Express would have been unimaginable.

ASIA

LEFT *The Nilagiri Express.*

By Bolan Mail to the Border

KARACHI TO CHAMAN, PAKISTAN

BY ANTHONY LAMBERT

ROUTE *Karachi–Quetta–Chaman, Pakistan.* **DISTANCE** *593km (369 miles).*
DURATION *Karachi–Quetta: 22 hours 20 minutes; Quetta–Chaman: 5 hours 15 minutes.* **GAUGE** *1676mm (5ft 6in).*

Of all the frontiers bordering British India, it was the western borders with unruly Afghanistan that caused the greatest anxiety and trouble. As a consequence, the region's railways were built mostly for strategic and military purposes, and much of the extraordinary line between Karachi, the largest city of today's Pakistan, and the Afghan border at Chaman falls into this category. It is easy to take the train as far as Quetta, the city that held the largest garrison in British India, but to venture beyond requires luck and perseverance.

Between Karachi and Quetta there is a choice of daily sleeping-car trains with such evocative names as the Sind Express and the Baluchistan Express, but it is the Bolan Mail, invoking the name of the pass through which armies have marched since the time of Alexander the Great, that best captures the romance of this wild and mountainous area. The 470km (292-mile) journey as far as Quetta takes roughly a day, but for trains over the final 123km (77 miles) to Chaman, the train service is subject to such uncertainties as the political circumstances of the region.

The journey is one of extreme contrasts, from the urban confusion of Karachi, across the oven of the Kachhi Plain to the desolate, snow-dusted mountain ranges that confined east–west movements to only a few passes. Even the construction of the railway ranged from terrain so easy that track-laying records were set to obstacles so challenging that two lines had to be abandoned in favour of a third attempt.

The solid masonry buildings at Karachi are typical of the major station construction that is also to be found throughout India, with no thought of producing anything cheap. The exit from Karachi takes in the usual cross-section of a city, moving through districts of varying affluence and order, until the train finally escapes into the flat countryside of the Sind, the province annexed by Sir Charles Napier in 1843. The railway between Karachi and Kotri was the first section of the route to be opened, in 1861, cutting out one of the most treacherous sections of the parallel Indus for steamer navigation.

Only the local stopping trains take the west-bank route out of the junction at Kotri, so trains bound for Quetta cross the mighty Indus river twice. The five-span bridge over the Indus at Kotri was not opened until 1900. It enabled faster trains to take the east-bank route to Rohri, thereby reducing the journey by 61km (38 miles) over the west-bank route. Directly across the bridge is the city of Hyderabad, which came into being because the Indus changed its course in the 18th century and flooded the then capital of the lower Sind. Such unpredictable floods have been the bane of civil engineers in this part of the world for centuries. From Hyderabad the line to Mirpur Khas heads east, once the fastest route to Delhi until border tensions curtailed operations, ending the chance to cross the Thar Desert by train.

LEFT *Throughout the Indian subcontinent, serious train overcrowding often leads to roof riding and the precarious clinging onto handrails, though in Pakistan this is usually confined to stopping trains.*

ABOVE *View from Mushkaf Tunnel No. 4 through to No. 6.*
LEFT *A 1950s ALCO diesel emerges from Pir Panjir Tunnel on the southern approach to the Dozan Gorge above Hirok. The crenellations are purely decorative, but a blockhouse was built to the right of the tunnel.*

The junction of Nawabshah may offer a glimpse of steam, as the line between here and Mirpur Khas is still worked by British-built locomotives from the 1920s. This is one of very few remaining lines anywhere in the world on which normal service trains are still worked by steam. At Rohri, Quetta-bound trains turn northwest to cross the Indus again, this time by a bridge opened in 1962 and built to the design of a New York consulting engineer, Dr. D.B. Steinman, who died just before it was completed. The Ayub Arch replaced one of the ugliest bridges ever built, the Lansdowne Bridge, which was the first bridge in India to use steel in its main load-bearing members. The Lansdowne Bridge was converted for lighter vehicular traffic. The train pauses at Ruk where the west-bank line from Kotri comes in from the south before pressing on to Jacobabad, named after General John Jacob, who commanded the Scinde Irregular Horse Regiment and became governor of Sind.

Leaving Jacobabad, the railway begins its crossing of the barren Kachhi desert, running in a dead straight line across the plain for over 160km (100 miles). The land is so flat that a locomotive headlight can be seen at night for 25km (15 miles), and there is nothing to break the monotony but a line of telegraph poles or the occasional camel. A terrible indication of the heat was given in 1915 when 32 ill-prepared British soldiers died of heatstroke on a troop train crossing this barren waste. Needless to say, the railway was built in the winter months, and quick work was made of it, the 215km (134 miles) between Ruk and Sibi being completed in just 101 days.

Sibi is one of the hottest places in Pakistan, and was the start of the problems for the railway's builders, for here the line has to climb from 140m (459ft) above sea level to a summit of 1780m (5840ft). Gradients of 1 in 25 were necessary, requiring up to four locomotives in steam days. But it was the way rivers – bone dry for months of the year – could become raging torrents in a mere matter of hours that destroyed the first two attempts to build a railway between Sibi and the summit of the line at Kolpur. Neither had been well engineered, so no half-measures were taken in the third effort, which produced a railway 'of a quality of engineering endeavour unsurpassed anywhere else in the world', to use the words of a civil engineer on the North Western Railway.

The numerous tunnels, viaducts and bridges that allow the railway to negotiate the twisting valleys north-west of Sibi were so well built that the masonry and steelwork have barely deteriorated. Both tunnel portals and bridge parapets have elegant crenellations, the longer tunnels having name- and date-plates set in the arch crowns. But this was not the first railway to reach Quetta; a single line from Sibi via Harnai had been opened in 1887, but it was prone to constant disruption through landslides, so a more dependable route through the Bolan Pass remained an objective. This, the third line between Sibi and Kolpur, was finally opened in 1897.

Not long after leaving Sibi the train is quickly dwarfed by the scale of the surrounding slopes and peaks, as the two diesel locomotives, front and rear, growl their way towards the Bolan Pass. Sidings veer off at crazily steep angles, protected by a pointsman standing with flags in hand beside a small lineside hut; these runaway spurs were designed to arrest the descent of a careering train in the unlikely event of the brakes failing. Every Sibi-bound train has to stop before the point at the runaway and sign the pointsman's book. However, even the steep gradient of these runaways did not prove sufficient on occasions: an eastbound train of Afghan fruit once hit a 0.4km (¼ mile) 1 in 8 catch siding at 60mph and went hurtling off the end. Between Sibi and Mach the line climbs into the barren foothills of the Central Brahui Range and through the Panir Tunnel, the longest on the Bolan. From Ab-i-Gum, where the double-track section begins, the trains climb at 1 in 33 for 11.2km (7 miles) to Mach where they reverse back into the curiously laid-out station. Its design was intended to allow northbound steam-hauled trains to accelerate rapidly on a level section of track before hitting the next gradient. Notices warned passengers not to attempt to board the train once it had started moving, so rapid was the acceleration.

ABOVE *The train for Quetta waits to leave Chaman. The extensive sidings were once the loading point for fruit grown in Afghanistan.*

For the 25km (15 miles) from Mach to the summit at Kolpur, the gradient is a steady 1 in 25, an astonishingly steep gradient for an adhesion railway of this gauge and exceeding anything found even in Switzerland. Sometimes four locomotives – two at the front and two pushing at the back – were required on heavy trains. The heat on the footplate in summer, with the fireman having to shovel ceaselessly to maintain steam pressure, must have been almost unbearable. At Hirok the valley begins to narrow, squeezing the railway into a precipitous defile with almost sheer walls of pale brown rock soaring above the line as it tunnels through or snakes round the bluffs and repeatedly leaps across the river, a torrent in spring and bone dry in summer. One of the tunnels is tellingly named Windy Corner; another Mary Jane after the wife of the railway's engineer.

Pausing briefly at the remote station of Kolpur, sheltered by a dozen stunted trees in a landscape where they are at a premium, the train passes through a tunnel that marks the transition from the pass to the plateau on which stands the town of Quetta, once the largest garrison of the Raj and still of military significance today. Spezand, the last station before Quetta, is the junction for the Nushki Extension railway that parallels the border between Baluchistan and Afghanistan to cross the frontier with Iran and terminate in Zahidan. Little of Quetta survived the devastating nocturnal earthquake of 1935 which killed 56,000 people in 25 seconds. The station was no exception, and a plaque on the new station commemorates the many staff of the North Western Railway who lost their lives. The cantonment area outside the town was largely spared, enabling soldiers to come to the relief of the ruined town and search for survivors in the rubble.

The railway on to Chaman was fully opened in 1892. It facilitated an improvement in the diet of India by speeding the distribution of fruit from Afghanistan in daily trains to the principal cities of Delhi, Madras and Bombay. It is still an artery for freight, though various plans – including a World Bank study – to increase its usefulness by extending it across Afghanistan to Tadzhikistan have, not surprisingly, come to nought.

Once the sprawling suburbs of Quetta have been left behind, the landscape takes on an almost surreal quality, with distant, pimply hills ranging in colour from pale cocoa to red beyond a sward of grass. This gives way to sun-bleached earth as the railway makes for the

Khojak Pass, which cuts through the south-western flank of the Toba Kakar hills. Atop the summits of many of the barren hills are defensive blockhouses, some three or four storeys tall, which guarded the passes against infiltration from the west.

The gruelling climb to the tunnel under the pass comes to a brief stop at Shelabagh station beside the southern portal to the longest tunnel in the Indian subcontinent, bored with the help of 65 Welsh tunnellers fresh from building the Severn Tunnel. The logistical problems of finding sufficient food and water for the several thousand workmen in such desolate country testifies to the technical and organizational abilities of the 19th-century engineers. Moreover, they had to contend with communication in more than a dozen languages, the workmen being drawn from as far afield as Tibet, Zanzibar and Persia. The 4km (2½-mile) long Khojak Tunnel required 19,764,426 bricks, which had to be fired near the site using coal mined near Sibi. Both portals of the Khojak Tunnel once boasted tall defensive towers and a permanent force of guards.

The summit is reached inside the tunnel, and the invariably wet rails required skilled driving to stop steam locomotives from slipping to a standstill. That is what happened in the 1920s when the Amir of Afghanistan was on his way to Britain on a state visit: unaccustomed to train travel, the Amir was unnerved by the dark and smoke in the tunnel. He panicked and pulled the alarm cord, bringing the train to a halt before the summit had been reached. It took the four locomotives 20 minutes to get the twelve-coach train underway again.

The train descends through a series of horseshoe curves with hazy views across the plain towards Afghanistan and journey's end at the border town of Chaman, where even the engine shed and adjacent water tower were built for defence, complete with crenellations and gun-loops. A huge supply of track materials was kept here during the Raj in case an extension over the final 107km (67 miles) to Kandahar was hastily required. It was never used, however, and the vital role of railways in warfare, which brought these lines into being, is today almost forgotten.

BELOW *Railway station scenes are of endless fascination to travellers in Pakistan, reflected in this animated group at Quetta.*

The Northern Railway of India

DELHI TO SIMLA, INDIA

BY PETER LEMMEY

ROUTE *Delhi Junction–Kalka–Barog–Simla, India.* **DISTANCE** *430km (267 miles).*
DURATION *fastest service 10 hours.* **GAUGE** *Delhi Junction–Kalka: 1676mm (5ft 6in) gauge, electric haulage;*
Kalka–Simla, 0.76m (2ft 6in) gauge, diesel-hauled train or rail motor car.

Travelling across India by train is an experience you are unlikely to forget. Whether you go by intercity express, or local train with wooden seats, rail travel in the subcontinent distills the Indian experience in a particularly memorable form. The vast railway network offers myriad opportunities for such journeys, often on schedules stretching several days at a time. However, for a foray from the capital that takes less than a day but packs in far more than its fair share of scenic and railway variety, you cannot do better than Northern Railway of India's route from Delhi to Simla.

Why should you head for a small town 430km (267 miles) away in the Himalayan foothills? After all, Delhi has a long list of attractions, chief among them its unmatched architectural heritage: Shah Jahan's vast 17th-century Red Fort and the British Imperial capital in New Delhi designed by Lutyens and Baker are world famous. In the Old City colourful markets and bazaars are awaiting exploration, and in the evening, where better than New Delhi for a cocktail on the lawn of a colonial-style Art Deco hotel?

Well, Simla's main allure may, perversely, be that it is so very unlike Delhi. The hill station's unpolluted air, mountain setting and generally unhurried atmosphere are a perfect antidote to the urban excitement of the capital – just the place for a weekend breather. The trip from Delhi requires no undue reserves of fortitude – at its fastest it takes barely 10 hours – yet at journey's end you are in sight of the western

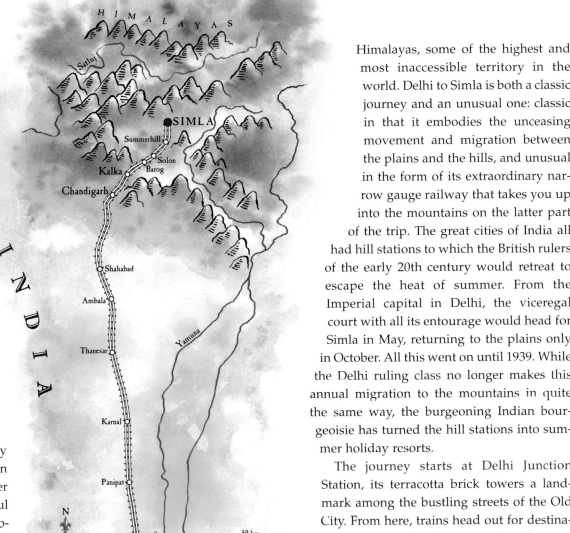

LEFT *On the Kalka to Simla narrow gauge line, a rail motor car pauses at picturesque Barog while the passengers take their breakfast in the station refreshment room (top right).*

Himalayas, some of the highest and most inaccessible territory in the world. Delhi to Simla is both a classic journey and an unusual one: classic in that it embodies the unceasing movement and migration between the plains and the hills, and unusual in the form of its extraordinary narrow gauge railway that takes you up into the mountains on the latter part of the trip. The great cities of India all had hill stations to which the British rulers of the early 20th century would retreat to escape the heat of summer. From the Imperial capital in Delhi, the viceregal court with all its entourage would head for Simla in May, returning to the plains only in October. All this went on until 1939. While the Delhi ruling class no longer makes this annual migration to the mountains in quite the same way, the burgeoning Indian bourgeoisie has turned the hill stations into summer holiday resorts.

The journey starts at Delhi Junction Station, its terracotta brick towers a landmark among the bustling streets of the Old City. From here, trains head out for destinations all over India. At any one time there are 11 million people making a journey on Indian Railways, and the first-time visitor walking in through Delhi Junction's arched entrance at peak hour may be forgiven for thinking that a good proportion of them are here on this station. However, crowded or not, the railway system is efficient and well organized; even the novice traveller will soon feel at home. The passengers are a cross-section of the subcontinent, colourfully attired country people rubbing shoulders with dapper businessmen. A small army of porters, vendors and hawkers also inhabits the station, moving from platform to platform as trains come and go.

The departure board at Delhi Junction contains temptations galore for travellers with time in hand, but for now we must resist the lure of trains like the Grand Trunk Express (to Chennai/Madras) or the Pink

Steaming into the Nilgiri Hills

MADRAS TO OOTACAMUND, INDIA

BY ANTHONY LAMBERT

ROUTE *Madras–Ootacamund, India.* **DISTANCE** *626km (389 miles).*
DURATION *16 hours.* **GAUGE** *1676mm (5ft 6in); 1m (3ft 3¹/₈in).*

Many train journeys start and finish in contrasting places, but few have had a greater resonance than those Indian journeys that took generations of grateful Britons from the heat of the plains to the cool of the mountains. This was not only a relief from discomfort; for many it was their last chance to reverse a potentially fatal illness. As the welcome sight of the Nilgiri Hills north of Coimbatore lifted their spirits, many hoped that the clean air of the 'Blue Mountains' would work the same magic as it did with one of its first European visitors: in 1819 the Naturalist to the King of France was almost at death's door when he accompanied the Collector of Coimbatore into these hills and recovered so miraculously that he was soon busy making a record of the area's distinctive flora.

Their destination was Ootacamund, situated at 2249m (7379ft) among the Nilgiri Hills that reach a height of almost 2578m (8458ft). Ooty, as it became known, was 'discovered' by Coimbatore's Collector, John Sullivan, after two of his assistants had described the upland area into which they had fled from smugglers. His passionate advocacy of the place gradually convinced others of its potential, and by the 1860s it had became the summer headquarters of the Madras government from April to October. The opening of the final section of the line must have come as an immense relief to the thousands involved in this annual migration. The metre gauge (3ft 3⅜in) railway opened in two stages: from the junction with the broad gauge (1676mm; 5ft 6in) at Mettupalaiyam to Coonoor in 1899, and on to Ooty in 1908.

LEFT *Almost there! En route from the humid heat of Madras to the cool relief waiting at Ootacamund, the train crosses this stout bridge over the Coonoor River on the section between Runneymede and Coonoor.*

It is in the often very humid heat of Madras (Chennai in Tamil) that the journey begins, perhaps by the overnight Nilagiri Express (the Southern Railway clings to the longer spelling), which has sleeping cars for Mettupalaiyam. Although few journeys by rail in India are without plenty to entertain the unfamiliar eye, there is nothing of distinction between Madras and Coimbatore, where the branch line to Mettupalaiyam leaves the Madras–Mangalore main line. So one misses little by covering the 374km (232 miles) in a bunk of an open-plan AC (air-conditioned) II 2-tier sleeping car, in which the opportunities for convivial conversation usually more than compensate for any lack of privacy. Their only drawback is the almost opaque tinted glazing of the windows.

The arcades of the broad gauge Central Station at Madras teem with passengers and porters, whose heads can carry as much as their arms. The semblance of chaos recalls the writings of that great observer of Indian life, the late James Cameron, who said that people don't visit railway stations in India, they inhabit them. But the reservation system seldom fails; even if stories of trains being a day late on a two-day schedule are not apocryphal, timekeeping is generally good.

It is worth rising at dawn and buying a cup of '*chai*' from a platform vendor at Coimbatore, where the train reverses, before finding a window seat in a non-AC first-class coach. For the branch to Mettupalaiyam, opened in 1873, offers the chance to watch the country come to life, as well as appreciating why the Nilgiris gained their nickname. At the red-tiled villages of small white-painted houses, dogs stretch and pigs begin their search for scraps while the stronger children heave on

AUSTRALIA

The Savannahlander

LEFT *Trestle bridge over the Copperfield River gorge at Einasleigh.*

The Savannahlander

CAIRNS TO FORSAYTH, QUEENSLAND, AUSTRALIA

BY PHILIP GAME

ROUTE *Cairns–Forsayth, Australia.* **DISTANCE** *423km (263 miles).*
DURATION *(Cairns to Almaden) 35 hours in total, with overnight stops at Almaden outbound,*
and Mount Surprise on return. **GAUGE** *1.06m (3ft 6in).*

Anthills, scrub, waving grass. The twin-carriage rail motor grinds to a halt on a deserted track. The engine driver beckons his few passengers. A breakdown? No, he's inviting us to step down and see the love-nest of a greater bowerbird, surrounded by gleaming gewgaws and shells. Where else could passengers disembark for a moment to admire a bird's nest; or share the engine driver's cabin, a vantage point from which the 1065mm (42in) narrow-gauge track seems a tenuous thread through the endless bush?

Flashback to 1992: on a warm tropical evening in Cairns, better known as the gateway to the Great Barrier Reef and the rainforests of the Daintree, a few intrepid enthusiasts board two antique carriages sandwiched between freight wagons and flat bed cars. Instead of hermetically sealed windows and vinyl seats we find old-fashioned wooden slats and genuine leather. Neither sleepers nor dining car are provided – we're laden with sleeping bags and provisions for the next 36 hours.

Once, this was the largest private railway network in Australia, traversing terrain rich in copper, gold, silver, lead, tin, wolfram (tungsten) and coal; ancient, convoluted rocks spiced with garnets, diamonds, rubies, sapphires and topaz. Until 1993 Mixed Goods 7A90 still climbed from Cairns up over the jungle-clad Great Dividing Range, then west into the scattered scrub of the Gulf Savannah country. Eventually, the 423km (263-mile) line to the tiny outback town of Forsayth, echoing through the 1950s to the thunder of ore and cattle trains, carried just one service a week.

No longer is the Forsayth train an obscure milk run. Launched in 1995, Queensland Rail's Savannahlander travels from Cairns to Forsayth, with overnight stops at Almaden near Chillagoe, and Mount

LEFT *The Savannahlander inches across Fossilbrook Creek, near Almaden, before stopping altogether to boil 'billy' for tea. On reaching Almaden an overnight halt is made for the excursion to the ghost town of Chillagoe.*

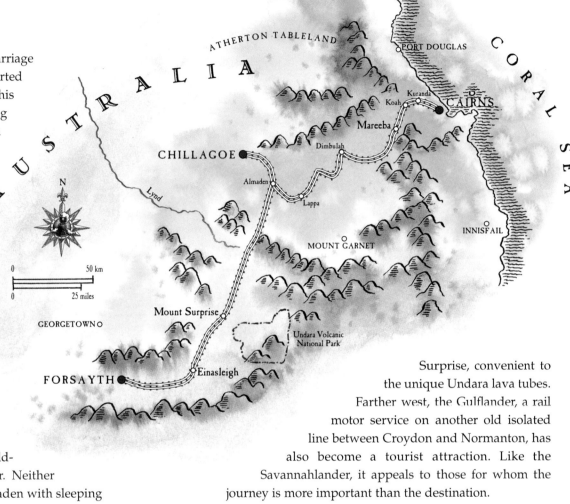

Surprise, convenient to the unique Undara lava tubes. Farther west, the Gulflander, a rail motor service on another old isolated line between Croydon and Normanton, has also become a tourist attraction. Like the Savannahlander, it appeals to those for whom the journey is more important than the destination.

Cairns at 6am. The old peach-pink timber station has been devoured by an omnivorous shopping complex and the new station is a featureless extension of its car park. Two gleaming bullet heads rumble alongside – refurbished 1960-vintage streamline rail motor units – basically old-fashioned coaches on rails that are less burdensome on rickety narrow-gauge tracks than a heavy locomotive.

As the sun rises the Savannahlander rattles through quiet streets of stilted, Queensland-style timber homes. Our route follows the popular tourist line up to Kuranda, through rainforests and across ravines. By mid-morning, day-trippers will be swarming onto the Kuranda Scenic Railway for the 90-minute run through emerald cane fields and the switchback climb up the sides of Barron Gorge. Perhaps a handful of them will notice that the rails continue inland. An army of heroic, if mostly nameless, Irish and Italian labourers carved out the 15 tunnels and countless culverts of the 'Cairns Range Railway'. Many of them dropped from malaria, dysentery, typhus, scrub ticks or snakebite.

Up on the Tablelands the mottled flanks of distant ranges loom over the sea of gently waving sugar cane that has supplanted the yellow

THE AUTHORS

TOM SAVIO says: 'My passion for railways began when I was four years old after an emergency trip to the hospital to set my broken arm. As a reward for my 'bravery' I was given a wind-up toy train. I literally ran its wheels off.

A year later, I took my first train ride over the rickety Long Island Rail Road to my grandmother's house. That trip has since been followed by a lifetime of train travel on five continents. Along the way I have served as stationmaster of a country depot, railway museum curator, rail travel consultant and even a steam locomotive driver on the Polish State Railways.

Photography was my other passion. Eventually, I combined my two loves, and my rail travel photographs and reminiscences have since been carried by the mainstream and enthusiast press and radio, and regularly in the pages of *International Railway Traveler* where I serve as Corresponding Editor. And still, I wake up each morning filled with the excitement of railways.'

Tom was both a contributor and the general editor of New Holland's *The World's Great Railway Journeys* published in 2001.

ANTHONY LAMBERT has written 15 books about railways and travel, including *Explore Britain's Steam Railways* and *Switzerland by Rail*. He contributed to the AA's *Train Journeys of the World*, *Insight Guide to Great Railway Journeys of Europe* and *Insight Guide to Pakistan*. He has also written for newspapers and magazines such as *The New York Times*, *The Daily Telegraph*, *The Sunday Times*, *Wanderlust* and the *Orient-Express Magazine*, was consultant editor to the nine-volume partwork *The World of Trains*, and a contributing author of *The World's Great Railway Journeys* published by New Holland in 2001.

ACKNOWLEDGEMENTS

TOM SAVIO thanks the following: Como. L.G. Arellanes, OWE; Eric Bélanger, progenitor of the Railway Baron appellation; Clifford Black, Amtrak Public Relations; Michael Brandt, White Pass & Yukon Route; Monica Campbell-Hoppé, Canadian Tourism Commission; A. Joel Frandsen, Butch Cassidy Historian; Chris Hillyard, RVM; Pippa Isbell, Orient Express Hotels & Trains; Jim Kemshead, Tourism Yukon; José Lafleur, Outaouais Tourism; Sueann Martell, Helper Mining & Railroad Museum; Elitsa Panayotova, Bulgarian Trade Office; Brian Rosenwald, Amtrak's California Zephyr; Lou Schuyler; and Sarducci's Cafe & Grill, San Juan Capistrano Station, 'where many an extraordinary railway journey was pondered over glasses of Chianti with my love mate, The Baroness Yvonne'.

ANTHONY LAMBERT wishes to acknowledge the assistance and kind cooperation of: Tim Bowcock, Carol Harris, Michael Helmerich, Chris McIntyre, David MacCallum-Price, David Mallender, Peter Mills, Roland Minder, Eve-Marie Morgo, Solenne Odon, Charles Page, Russell Palmer, Patricia de Pouzilhac, Eddie Toal, Carol Tumber, Elaine Wilde. Railway and travel companies: Air France, First Great Western, GNER, Rail Europe, Rhätische Bahn, ScotRail, Sunvil Africa, Swiss Federal Railways and Switzerland Tourism. In France: The Hotel Mermoz (Toulouse) and Auberge de Cèdre (Villefranche de Conflent); Namibia: The Hilltop House (Windhoek) and Swakopmund Hotel; and in Switzerland: La Margna (St Moritz).

INDEX

158